ROBERT MERRITT (1945–2011) was brought up on Erambie Aboriginal Mission, New South Wales. *The Cake Man*, written in isolation in Bathurst, was an attempt to express the root causes of Aboriginal despair. It was first performed in 1975 by the newly-formed Black Theatre in Redfern, followed by a number of successful productions. In 1982, *The Cake Man* received standing ovations when it premiered at the World Theatre Festival in Denver, Colorado. In 1984, Robert Merritt founded the Eora Centre for the Visual and Performing Arts (Eora College) in Redfern, for the purposes of providing training in the arts to Aboriginal students. Throughout the 1980s he made a number of documentary films, was Chair of the Aboriginal Arts Board, the first Aboriginal member of the Australia Council, and Chair of the Festival of Pacific Arts in 1988. Robert died in May 2011.

Dialogue
Talkin' life with brother Jim,
Tell 'im where's the pain.
Shake 'im word stick at my mind,
Helps me see it plain.

—R.J.M

The
Cake
Man

Robert Merritt

CURRENCY PRESS
The performing arts publisher

CURRENCY PLAYS

First published in 1978
by Currency Press.
Gadigal Land, Suite 310, 46–56 Kippax Street, Surry Hills, NSW 2010, Australia
enquiries@currency.com.au
www.currency.com.au

This revised edition first published in 2024.

Typeset by Brighton Gray for Currency Press.
Cover design by Jo Hunt; cover illustration by Dub Leffler.

Currency Press acknowledges the Traditional Owners of the Country on which we live
and work. We pay our respects to all Aboriginal and Torres Strait Islander Elders, past and
present.

Contents

ACKNOWLEDGEMENTS

We are indebted to the following for kind permission to quote from works under copyright: Barry Craze, for his *The Wiraqjuri Tribe Aborigines on the Lachlan-and their contact with explorers and settlers*; Paul Coe, Vera Lovelock and editor Colin Tatz for *Black Viewpoints, the Aboriginal Experience*, ANZ Book Company, Sydney, 1975; Stewart Harris and the Australian National University Press for *This Our Land*.

A NOTE ON SPELLING AND LANGUAGE

Spelling has been updated within introductions, *Another World* and *A Mystery of Infinite Complexity*, from the 1978 publication to acknowledge language shifts in regards to Aboriginal and Torres Strait Islander peoples.

The author's preface and any direct quotes within the introductions, however, have not had their spelling changed. The playscript retains its original spelling from 1978.

Author's Preface to the Second Edition

Theatre for us, the offspring of a once proud people who bred great artists, dates back to our rightful place in time, before our dreaming was shattered some two hundred years ago. It was part of the natural way. We inherited it from the womb and relied on it to reflect our spirit because it gave continuity to our existence. It told us all we needed to know, that there was no beginning and there was no end. It moulded our identity and carried our culture from generation to generation. From it we took for granted the fact that we belonged.

But today in multi-racial Australia the artistic arena makes little attempt to understand the alienated position of Aboriginal people within the wider Australian community. The film industry, that by-product of the theatre, holds the power to create images and ideals that undoubtedly influence societies and mould our everyday existence—and yet it does nothing positive in its depiction of indigenous Australians. Audiences both here and overseas have been and are being deprived of a chance to share our cultural background. Projects in which Aboriginal people have been involved, in any capacity other than as actors, have been confined to the experimental. The history of *The Cake Man* has been its emergence from the experimental into the mainstream of white-dominated professional theatre.

In 1975 I had the privilege of giving the old Black Theatre in Redfern the opportunity to perform my play. Unfortunately for them they had no credibility in the eyes of the public funding bodies: they were reduced to giving a workshop treatment only. Nevertheless the exercise served its purpose: audiences, both black and white, found their way into the black domain.

In 1977 the play was secured by the Australian Broadcasting Commission for national television. I capitalised upon the opportunity by submitting an application to the Aboriginal Arts Board of the Australia Council for funds for a professional stage production. At that time it was to be all-black. The Board offered us $12,000. I was disillusioned: I knew I wouldn't get what I wanted on this amount. Soon after that I met George Ogilvie, then the most renowned theatre director in the land, who had just ended his contract with the South Australian Theatre Company. He not only liked the play but saw it as a fresh challenge. We submitted a more realistic budget to the Aboriginal Arts Board. It was successful and the production opened at the Bondi Pavilion Theatre in Sydney, on 30 April 1977. Audiences, both black and white, came from all over the country into the white domain.

After the Bondi season, invitations for the play came from all over Australia and overseas. Producers were approached and applications submitted to various funding bodies. But, because our Aboriginal characters were not from the Stone Age, black theatre was not seen as a commercial proposition. Al Grassby, then Commissioner for Community Relations for the Federal Government, wrote on 7 June 1977 to Harry M Miller, the well-known entrepreneur, who had been appointed Chairman of the Queen's Jubilee Commemorative Organisation with one million dollars to spend. Grassby urged Miller to use Jubilee funds to tour *The Cake Man* around the country and play it in London, the Jubilee imperial capital. There was no more worthwhile project, he argued, than a production which depicted Australian history over two hundred years. The answer, understandably, was 'No'. The Committee opted instead to light bonfires around Australia and display the Queen's coronation carriage.

In 1981, Aboriginal theatre raised its frustrated head again in hope when renewed interest in *The Cake Man* came from overseas. The artistic director of the Australian Elizabethan Theatre Trust, Anthony Steel, was approached and his response was encouraging. The following year the Trust gave an undertaking to raise the pre-production costs for an American-Canadian tour which would include the World Theatre Festival in Denver, Colorado, in July 1982, where the play would officially represent Australia, along with Ron Elisha's *Einstein* from the Melbourne Theatre Company.

The Trust made approaches to various funding bodies. The response was negative, despite all the letters of support we had gathered from politicians of the two major parties. The Trust sent out 140 letters to private companies (with an emphasis on those with American parentage) asking for a donation of $500, tax deductible under Section

78 (l)(A) of the Income Tax Act. The Trust promised acknowledgement of donor's sponsorship in promotional material used in connection with the tour. There was only one positive response: The Commercial Banking Company of Sydney donated $500.

The Trust informed the Aboriginal Theatre Company of the financial situation and said they would have to withdraw as their constitution allowed them to support Australian content only within Australia. They were therefore cancelling the North American tour. There remained only four hours in which to confirm our participation in the World Theatre Festival.

It was, however, the Aboriginal Theatre Company who had signed the contract with Denver. I telephoned the Festival Director, Al Kraizer, and told him we were going it alone. I just couldn't believe it. We had had bestowed on us the highest honour in the theatre and we were reduced to becoming beggars to get there. Father Alan Mithen, of the Pallottine Fathers and Brothers of Australia, and other Catholic orders supported us to the pre-production stage. The Shadow Minister for Aborigines and the Arts, Senator Susan Ryan, asked some questions in Parliament. In the meantime the Trust agreed to stick with us.

After making the rounds of the hand-out traps we received contributions from the Aboriginal Arts Board, the Department of Foreign Affairs, the New South Wales Government through the Premier's Department and the Australian Elizabethan Theatre Trust, who set up a three performance warm-up season at the Parade Theatre, Sydney.

The Aboriginal Theatre Company didn't know it at the time but half our $11,000 performing fee had been paid to the Elizabethan Theatre Trust before we arrived in America. After the season in Denver we noble natives decided to let the Trust have the whole of the fee. We felt we had made our point.

In America I soon discovered what national pride was all about. When asked by another director: 'Where's your flag?', I realised that from thirteen different countries our Australian Aboriginal Theatre was the only one without a flag. I felt the meaning of his words and he knew it. 'You're looking at it', was my reply.

The fact that the whole season in Denver sold out before the opening performance gave us little sense of security at the outset. Before I left

Australia I had been advised strongly to include notes of explanation
in the programme, lest audiences fail to understand the play. I watched
the audience reaction very closely and was soon reassured. They read
the play's message crystal clear.

Their appreciation of the performances by the three talented
Aboriginal artists, Justine Saunders (Ruby), Brian Syron (Sweet
William) and Graham Moore (Pumpkinhead), in some of the most
demanding roles in the Australian repertoire, was demonstrated in
standing ovations after every performance. It made us, brought up in
the shadow of two hundred years of repression, for the first time value
our own worth. In retrospect I cannot help but shudder at the memory
of that raggedy-arsed bunch of people who crept into the international
arena in Denver on a $60,000 budget that smelt of last-minute shame,
and then stood up in the company of greats to be counted.

In Melbourne, after the post-U.S. season had already been extended
at the Universal Theatre, the company had the choice of extending still
further or going on to Brisbane to part of the Warana-Commonwealth
Arts Festival. The Festival won out. The season in Brisbane was
funded by the then Minister for Aboriginal Affairs, Ian Wilson. History
teaches us that the way to genocide is to take a culture, mould it into
a defunct company—bankrupt, at the mercy of the liquidators—and
destroy its credibility so it can no longer reflect itself. The consoling
thought to come out of the *Cake Man* tour is that whatever struggle
for recognition may have gone into its realisation, up there on stage
we were judged by audiences both here and in the U.S. on our own
individual talent, not on our colour.

Sydney, 1983

Another World

Twenty years ago, the Erambie Aboriginal mission station at Cowra was very much on the wrong side of the Lachlan River. Not that crossing the river from east to west was, by itself, regarded as being all that bad. It depended on who you were, where you were going and what you expected to find when you got there.

If you were a white citizen with some sort of steady income, then crossing the Lachlan usually meant having fun. The local show, horse races, picnic race ball, dog races, the trots (a famous breeding centre: Lawn Derby and progeny raced here amongst others), rugby league, cattle and sheep sales and the beautiful golf course with the snake pit club house where many a relationship began and ended; these were the facilities for which most west-bound travellers searched. A small portion of the white population actually lived at West Cowra—but this was mainly because the Housing Commission had once built some houses to provide cheap rents and others had followed.

At the time I went to Cowra as a young policeman in 1958 West Cowra had a small shopping centre but no doctor, dentist or any similar specialist luxuries. On the other hand, about ninety-nine per cent of Cowra's black population lived there: either on the mission itself or on a vacant block of ground nearby. Those on the vacant block were there because either they or a close relative had been 'barred' from the mission.

During this period the mission was administered by a body called, as I recall, the Aboriginal Welfare Board, under the direct control of a superintendent. As well as having the power to 'expel' badly behaved residents, the mission superintendents liked the company of police. Either that or they saw the welfare of the people under their control and the work rate of the local police as interdependent. For, whatever the reason, few 'incidents' on the mission passed without a call to the police. Cowra, being a close knit town, meant there was no escape from such calls for the unfortunate on duty. Even the back row of the picture theatre on the coldest night was not safe.

And so as a young policeman I was instantly enveloped in a routine which took it for granted that there would be regular visits and regular arrests at the mission. For a while the routine did not worry me too much, apart from being time-consuming. But bit by bit the unfairness of the situation and the sheer irrelevancy of the police approach began to tell. Two aspects of my work gradually got right under my skin and became the start of my social conscience. The first was the difference in the law as it applied to blacks and whites. There is no time to deal with all the distinctions but the law regarding liquor, for example, was impossible. A person with 'an apparent admixture of native blood' was forbidden to drink liquor at all. At Cowra we did not worry about this too much but as a law it was generally enforced. The biggest source of jail cargo, however, was a by-law that provided a penalty of ten pounds ($20) for anyone found on the mission 'under the influence of alcohol'. To make the distinction clear, the law also provided for a fine of two pounds ($4) for being drunk in a public street.

The practice then was to release any drunk who could raise ten shillings' bail after he had been in custody for four hours or until he sobered up. No-one worried if he did not turn up to collect his ten shillings and face the magistrate. Thus, in town, a white man could get bombed out of his mind for a four hour trip to the jug and ten bob. A black who bought his grog and safely smuggled it across the river to the mission only had to be found 'under the influence' around his own home and the fine was ten pounds.

The enforcement of these different laws for different degrees of the same offence was the second matter that angered me. Blacks in my recollection were invariably fined the maximum ten pounds. Not having this money they had to cut it out at the rate of ten shillings a day—the same as the white man paid for his four hours. It is sad to say that in 1977, although the law is now the same for black and white, in many western river towns it is still the black man who is arrested and it is still the black man who gets the maximum sentence.

One day in 1959, I had to cross the river to go to the racecourse, but not to bet. Word had been received of a burglary and at, no doubt, great risk to anyone in our way, I and another policeman set out to apprehend the offenders. Near the course proper we found four young black boys, each drinking a bottle of lemonade. They had pulled some wire away from the racecourse bar to obtain same, so naturally they were each charged with breaking and entering. Later in court, determined to stamp this practice out, the visiting magistrate imposed a less-than-light sentence. One of those boys was Robert J. Merritt.

Robert and his brother, Kevin, appealed against their sentence. To assist His Honour, Judge Holt, it fell to me to prepare a report on the environment of the appellants. The report did not flatter the administration of the Aboriginal Welfare Board. In court I expounded further and agreed with counsel for Robert and his brother that they had little chance to obtain such luxuries as lemonade without stealing. Their sentence was reduced. On my return to Cowra I was directed to report and further asked what had possessed me to give such evidence. The chance enabled me to give the Board a second serve on the subject of what I regarded as the shocking results of its policies no matter how well meaning they may have been.

My major memories of the Erambie mission of those times were of just how tough life was for most of the residents. It was a time of recession and many Cowra people were out of work. Even now I remember that Gordon Simpson had a regular job with the Council and Lindsay Coe had one with the railways. A young man, Kennedy, had a regular job in town—and that was it. Droving, shearing, asparagus cutting, wheat and lucerne lumping brought a few quid to some families, but many simply depended on welfare. And no matter what is said about pensions these days, in the 1950s they were designed to encourage the recipients to work. Cowra just did not have enough work to go around.

In winter, it is a cold town. In fact it is a town of extreme temperatures. One summer it touched 112 degrees Fahrenheit: the local newspaper reported birds dropping out of the trees in the River Park. You get under a tree or a shelter or you dive in the river and get away from the heat; but the cold is relentless and permits only those with property to escape it. I remember it once hit nineteen degrees and the deep main street gutters were covered with ice: very much four blanket weather in bed and a big fire last thing at night and early in the morning. Not surprisingly fuel did not last long at Erambie. The chainsaw and the truck had long since denuded the mission area of dry timber. Everything from railway sleepers to newspapers and even floorboards were burnt in order to keep the cold at bay for a few moments more.

But there was plenty of spirit and companionship at Cowra in spite of the crushing poverty. One old sparring partner of mine, Cameron Bamblett, used to say that if he was warm inside he was warm all over. He usually managed to stay warm inside. A highly skilled drover himself, he contrived to get arrested for things that are never heard of these days: riding a horse while under the influence, riding a bicycle in the same condition, driving a horse and sulky in a dangerous manner— and so on. Because they stayed forgotten on the statute books as relics of another era, no-one had bothered to upgrade the fine. Cameron used openly to boast that the trivial amount it cost him was well invested against the times he got away with it.

But in times of crisis, the Erambie Aboriginal people knew how to stick together. One fine New Year's Day, a family and friends went on a picnic to the river bank. The father was swimming when a few yards from shore he suddenly put his hands up and sank. Somewhat eerily he was found a day later in much the same spot but under a log about fifteen feet down. It was a very difficult place for a good swimmer to reach if he tried. The incident revived stories of Dreamtime spirits of the river. It also meant problems for the family: a young widow and a number of very young daughters. The mob stuck together and weathered that terrible storm.

Most of the matters here would be unknown to the whites of that period in Cowra. For them at that time it was not an area a few hundred metres from where they played—but another world.

Robert Merritt's play *The Cake Man* depicts with accuracy in dramatic form a past way of life as we both remember it from when he was growing up in the 1960s. It is still the present for too many people in Australia.

Mervyn Rutherford

A Mystery of Infinite Complexity

An aspect of Aboriginal life seen through the eyes of a European, 1813: *Smoking out the Opossum,* J. H. Clark, 1750–1849. From the Nan Kivell Collection, reproduced by kind permission of the Australian National Library.

Cowra, which provides the setting for *The Cake Man,* is a medium sized country town in the Central Western district of New South Wales: an area which has had an ambivalent history of race relations. From the time the first European settlers crossed the Blue Mountains to cultivate the land beyond there were incidents of theft and murder and the spread of disease among the Aboriginal people. And this continued throughout the century.

It was in the 1840s that the British Government first began to reserve land for the Aboriginal people. The thirty-one acres at Erambie, on the east bank of the Lachlan River on the edge of the Cowra township was declared an Aboriginal reserve in 1890 and in the early part of the new century became a mission under the jurisdiction of the Aboriginal Welfare Board. It remained so until 1965 when the manager was transferred and it became a reserve under police supervision. Barry Craze, a conservationist and member of the Cowra Historical Society, has gathered together a portrait of early relations between the Wiradjuri tribe, whose land stretched along the Lachlan River, and the whites[1] who came to settle. Robert Merritt is a descendant of the Wiradjuris, whose name means 'No'. The early explorers[2] found the country rich with kangaroos and emus, platypus, rabbit-eared bandicoots, dingoes, cockatoos and crows, swans, black duck, teal and wild turkeys. The huge tribal lands of the Wiradjuris, writes Craze:

.. extended from the Murray River in the south to between the Lachlan and Macquarie rivers in the north, the west by these rivers and east by the Highlands. Over the vast area they roved, adjusting their movement to the hunting and gathering cycle. They could

melt into the landscape and not be observed, and Cunningham and Oxley both noted seeing camp-fires but no aborigines near them.

A more significant proof of their integration into the environment was their effective conservation of its resources, for they lived in harmony with their environment—animal, bird and plant life. They took no more food than they required, and, by their nomadic habit, they never outfished or outhunted the areas. They did, however, set light to the country at times to foster fresh grass regrowth, thus making ideal browsing conditions for kangaroo and emu.

The attitude of the Aboriginal people to the white intruders was first one of fear, writes Craze and he quotes G. W. Evans in his journal on 28 May 1815, when camping near the site of the present town of Cowra:

We see the natives two or three times a day; I believe we are a great terror to them; a woman with a young child fell in our way this afternoon, to whom I gave a tomahawk and other trifles; she was glad to depart; soon after we suddenly came upon a man who was much frightened; he ran up a tree in a moment, carrying with him his spear and crooked throwing stick; he bellowed and cried out so much and so loud, that he might have been heard half a mile; it was useless entreating him to come down, therefore stuck a tomahawk in the tree and left him; the more I spoke the more he cried out.[3]

The first clash with the Europeans occurred in 1817, according to Craze, at the depot on the Lachlan at Soldiers' Flat, set up for the purpose of equipping John Oxley's expedition the following year. Aborigines had run off with a pair of muskets and in the chase an Aboriginal boy was shot. About this time members of the Wiradjuri tribe near Bathurst began taking and killing stock. Craze writes:

The settlers had occupied land on which the Aborigines had roamed and hunted for food, but more importantly some of the new farms included areas of great social and sacred significance to the Aborigines. The settlers were regarded as intruders and their dogs and firearms were already frightening off the game on which the Aborigines depended, and whose sheep and cattle would deplete and destroy much of the vegetable food on which they relied. Later in 1822 William Lawson reported the killing of one of his convicts by the Aborigines. In September 1823 a shepherd hutkeeper was killed ten miles from Bathurst, and in October and November Aborigines attacked several stations, killing some shepherds and stock keepers, and scattering and spreading sheep and cattle. The Government station at Swallow Creek was abandoned and the herds brought back to Bathurst. Finally on 24th August 1824 Governor Brisbane proclaimed martial law over the country 'westward of Mt 'York', in an attempt to quell the trouble. To enforce the decree a detachment of the 40th Regiment was rushed to Bathurst to bring the total number of soldiers stationed there to 75. These men, augmented by a number of armed settlers, began a systematic campaign of terror and murder against the Aborigines.

After two months, Aboriginal peoples began to enter Bathurst peaceably and the Proclamation was repealed on 11 December 1824.

It was not only by violence and starvation that the blacks were dying, however. Tuberculosis, venereal disease and a malady akin to smallpox with a mortality rate that 'varied from one in three to one in five or six', according to Craze, all made heavy depredations upon the population.

He estimates the Wiradjuri numbers in 1830 at between 1,000 and 1,500. Relations between the black nomadic and white agricultural ways of life having begun in mutual incomprehension and grown in mutual antipathy, the British Government attempted in the 1840s to retrieve matters by setting aside reserves on which the blacks could settle. The failure of these attempts, Craze points out, is obvious from the annual report made in 1853 by the Commissioner of Crown Lands, Edgar Beckham on *The State of Aborigines in the Lachlan District:*

During the year 1853 I have taken every opportunity of making known to the Aborigines that tracts of land have been set apart for their especial use; but I do not think there is any prospect of the natives availing themselves of those reserves until such time as some further inducement is held out to them to do so—and I would beg leave to suggest that Government Establishments should be formed upon the Reserves alluded to under the Superintendence of a Resident Protector or Governor which I think would induce the natives to locale upon these lands and eventually bring them into a state of Civilization.

Thus began the policy of paternalism today seen as a principal root
cause of the destruction of our Aboriginal culture. Beckham goes on:

*The Aborigines inhabiting this district are a quite well conducted
race at all times evincing a good feeling towards the Europeans.
They have generally but little inclination for normal labour but I
have known them to be much service to the settlers at sheep washing
and during the harvest. Payment of their labour is usually made in
rations and clothes, but I have invariably found that they would
work more willingly for money than anything else. There are some
few of the Aborigines employed as stockmen, for which service they
are well adapted, they are fond of riding and remarkably quick in
distinguishing the stock belonging to their master to those of other
parties.*

After the 1850s, says Craze, there is little surviving documentation
about the Lachlan Aboriginal clan.

The dearth was probably due to the universal acceptance at this time
of the conviction that Aboriginal peoples were a dying race. However
it is known that the Aboriginal people continued to live next to the
West Cowra Recreation Ground by the river and in 1890 the Erambie
reserve of 31 acres was declared. By 1891, 43 Aboriginal people were
camped there and a special school for Aboriginal peoples opened in
1893.

The Erambie Mission in the 1950s and early 1960s when Robert
Merritt was growing up there, was, on the evidence, no worse than
most such reserves. There was poverty and social welfare cheques and
drunkenness and a sense of defeat. Merritt went first to the mission
primary school and then to the primary and secondary schools in the
town. According to *his* contemporaries he was a bright student who
excelled both at schoolwork and athletics. But he wagged school and
at fifteen dropped out.

Here are two views of school as Aboriginal peoples remember it at
that time. Michael Anderson, who was brought up in Walgett:

*When the white man first came to Australia he tried to push the
Aborigine into becoming a white man. It didn't work. Today they
still do the same thing to Aboriginal children. Unfortunately for the
Aboriginal child he cannot become white: because of the colour*

of his skin and because of his background. Today's education system teaches us how to make planes and cars, how to make a lot of money. But I don't see any value in that. When I was going to school, we used to look at each other's books—the teacher used to smack us on the knuckles with a ruler and say that's bad, don't do that. I'll tell you why we did it. In the Aboriginal community we shared knowledge, we tried to help each other. We didn't try to put each other down. It was strange to me to have to hide my little piece of paper: that was when I started getting all mixed up.[4]

Kevin Gilbert, now a writer and poet who grew up at Narrandera, N.S.W., in the 1950s gave this moving account to the Senate Standing Committee on Social Environment in 1975:

[…] and then we get the white teacher. He doesn't understand the psychology of that black child in his classroom. He doesn't understand the way in which he, through his school teaching, attacks the psychology of that child, poisons that child. He gets that little black kid to stand up with the rest of the class and sing: 'In 1779 we ploughed the loam in our newfound home amongst the eucalyptus trees' and he gets that kid to stand up and say Joe Mope and Bill Slope were the first men to cross the Blue Mountains. He gets the little black kid to stand up and sing glory Australia, advance Australia fair and he talks about justice and hope and the wonderful sunburnt country to that kid who has just seen the police burst into his mother's bedroom and drag his father out of bed and give him a belt in the mouth […] carting him off to jail for some petty crime. That teacher didn't see the police come out and round up all the kids' pet dogs on the mission and shoot them all and leave the bodies smelling in the sun […] the kids know that they're always only talking about justice for whites. The teacher talks about England and Germany and Europe and the countries of the world. And he talks then about Australia. Of how it was discovered and how the blacks were primitive and how the great white race pushed these savages […] And he gives the little black kids picture books to read: about Jack and the Beanstalk, about Alice in Wonderland and the legends that came from Europe, the legends written by whites. Sooner or later he gives the little black kid a book about Aboriginal

legends, written by whites. Little campfire stories, passed off as the grown-up, living legends of a people. With all the romance, all the understanding, all the love, all the Law, all the life stripped out of the guts of it by whites. And then the whites say that the only chance that Aborigines have is in education![5]

But the worst aspect of mission life in the experience of those who have written about it, was the white 'protection' that sapped at the blacks' independence. Paul Coe of the Aboriginal Legal Service, a former Rugby League star and one of a large family brought up with Merritt on Erambie Mission, puts it this way:

The blacks in New South Wales, over a period of fifty years, have been forced to live under what I call managerial suppression. The Government had decided that the blacks would be put out on mission stations. The land they were located on was usually of no value. I was brought up on one myself. You had to lose your selfrespect entirely because in order to do anything you had to ask the manager for permission. He was the big 'bwana' figure, father and ogre. For fifty years they didn't let their 'children' grow up.[6]

Following a referendum in 1967 at which the people of Australia voted in favour of the Commonwealth taking over legislation relating to Aboriginal affairs from the States, the Aborigines Welfare Board was disbanded. Two new bodies were set up: an Advisory Council for Aboriginal Affairs and an Office of Aboriginal Affairs, to lay down policy and implement it through the relevant State departments. Erambie was handed over to the Lands Trust and from there to a Kuri Housing Company established at Cowra. The records of the mission, which tell a revealing story of current white attitudes, became Aboriginal property[7] and we have permission here to quote from some of them. Names have been changed in courtesy to those involved.

On 9 June 1955 the then Superintendent of the Aborigines Welfare Board wrote to the manager at Erambie in the matter of blankets:

Mrs Anne Jones of Cowra has made application for blankets for one three-quarter bed and two single beds. She states that she has five children; her husband is a drover but averages only about two days work each week. Please furnish a report and recommendation regarding the support of blankets to Mrs Jones, stating the husband's weekly income and any other income received in the household: caste, general character, etc.

The manager replied:

I have to advise that the abovementioned and her family are Lesser Castes. The husband is a drover, horsebreaker, deadwool gatherer and according to information a gatherer of anything when no-one is looking. If Jones can only average two days work a week, it is his laziness, as all other drovers work most of the year, it is a very lucrative business.

I interviewed Jones at their residence and asked to be shown the beds for which they required these blankets. There was only one bed in the house supported by drums. I asked where the other beds were, I was told in Sydney!

Mrs Jones has five children of a fair colouring and whom I have never seen clean. The children could do with the blankets and I suggest that a monthly check be made of the blankets as they are liable to be converted to coin.

The Board refused the Jones family their blankets.

In 1959 the case of Robert and Kevin Merritt referred to in Mervyn Rutherford's introduction drew local attention to conditions at Erambie. On 19 June 1959 the Aborigines Welfare Board Superintendent, referring to the case being remanded until 26 June, made this request of the manager:

Will you please let me have your comment, before that date, on the statement made by Constable Rutherford, when giving his evidence, that living conditions on the Aboriginal Station, Cowra, are lower than in the worst slum areas in Sydney. Constable Rutherford also stated that immorality was rife and, that, generally speaking, the whole Station environment was bad.

The manager made his report on 22 June:

From the Statement made by Constable Rutherford before Judge Holt in No. 2 Appeal Court on 11th June 1959, it would appear that he was prepared to make any statement that would prevent the Merritt boys from returning with their Parents to Cowra.

Constable Rutherford has, to my knowledge, visited the Station on only two occasions since November 1958. He is well aware that the Aborigines of this Station have given little cause for complaint, either to myself as Manager of the Station, or the Cowra Police. Since November on four occasions only have Residents been charged with being under the Influence on the Station. And there has been only one case of immorality to my knowledge, or to the knowledge of Rutherford' s Senior Officers of the Cowra Police, from whom I made enquiry today.

In reference to the slum conditions alleged by Rutherford, there are 127 Aborigines on the Station, they are housed in four twobedroom cottages, and sixteen three-bedroom Cottages; in addition there is a single men's quarters of eight rooms. As there is only one family to each Cottage, there is no overcrowding, and all Cottages have a separate yard fenced in, where in season the Residents have in most cases nice Gardens.

The Station is frequently inspected by the local Health Inspector, as it is within the Municipal boundary of Cowra, and his reports as to the cleanliness of the homes and the general condition of the Station have been excellent. There are sixteen able-bodied men Resident on the Station. Eleven are in employment, five are not permanently employed but do casual work such as gardening and day labouring jobs.

The Station is visited twice weekly by members of the United Aborigines Mission who in addition hold a Church Service each Sunday and also conduct a Sunday School. Deaconess Johnson of the Presbyterian Church also visits twice weekly and conducts organised play for the Children and Father O'Reilly of the Catholic Church makes frequent visits to the Station, serves Mass in the Chapel once a month, keeps all children who attend the Convent School up to the mark with their attendance. All of these Church people are very happy with the result achieved by their efforts. Which indicates that the environment is good.

The care of the children was a matter of concern to local residents. One woman, after hearing a radio broadcast about the Aboriginal children at Cowra School having no lunch, offered to supply hot soup and other help. As she is registered with the Child Welfare as a child minder, she writes:

> *I would like to offer to take the Baby, or if you had a Child that needed building up with good food and Care, of any of the things that arise out of try to bring up a family. Say an unmarried Mother that would like to keep her baby and wanted time to get work. Or any of those things.*

The Welfare Board had the following view of the efforts of the Country Women's Association, who had:

> *[...] undertaken to adopt Mary Brown of this station in their effort to help her to be assimilated into the white community. Their attention was drawn to Mary as a result of her examination marks in the half-yearly exams. Mary achieved first place in her class. In their effort to help Mary the C.W.A. have offered to supply her with all school clothing and requisites. They have arranged outings for her with their children and they will remember her at such times as birthdays and Christmas. Mary is by nature a quiet retiring child but she seems to be responding to these efforts very well.*

Mary was ten years old at that time. Meanwhile Elsie Donovan, three years older, was not faring so well.

> *Reference case: Elsie Donovan aged 13 years, lesser caste. Charged on three occasions, stealing once, destroying private property, non attendance at school without good and proper reason, self admittance to knowledge of many men. Placed on 12 month bond. She broke the Bond after one week. Threatened to burn down the home, if instant action was not taken she would have burnt the home. Girl was arrested and committed to the care and control of the Minister.*

Not everyone could live on Erambie. Those who wished to apply for residence had to declare an admixture of Aboriginal blood and residence in N.S.W. for at least six months. The decision was made by the Welfare Board in Sydney based on reports of means and good character. An unemployed white man married to a black woman was refused permission to reside with his family on the ground that he should provide a home for his family off the station. Occasionally efforts were made to find employment for the residents. On 2 November 1964 the Welfare Board Superintendent issued a circular to field staff following a welfare officers' conference suggesting that the example of the Department of Native Affairs in Queensland be followed in 'utilising natural skills of Aborigines within the State in boomerang making and curio making'. He added 'It will be appreciated that in a competitive market good quality products only could be considered.' The report from Erambie was revealing:

> *The residents of this Station are very capable of making a variety of First Class products for sale as curios, but it has been found that first class work does not sell anywhere near the same as crude work, i.e. a beautiful wall plaque, designed, made, baked, coloured and glazed to perfection, could not be sold at our Fete as it was thought to be factory made; yet a crude affair with thumb prints and indentations was snapped up. It therefore follows that the production of good quality items must compete with factory work, whereas the public look for and accept beautiful but crude work from Aborigines. It is the opinion of the people of this Station that they can only cope with local demand which is high.*

Today things are much the same at Erambie except that there is no 'bwana'. Money has been made available neither through the black nor the white organisations to improve the standard of housing. At the time of publication a sewerage system sunk with money from the housing company had lain unused for eighteen months awaiting funds to connect it to the houses. Meanwhile bath and sink water runs from broken drains and the nightman still called on the ricketty outhouses. Now the blacks are free to leave, the young ones go—to the Sydney ghettoes in Redfern, Waterloo, Alexandria and Newtown. But the old ones have stayed on. Vera Lovelock, health officer in Aboriginal communities for the N.S.W. Health Commission explains why:[8]

> *[…] the hard and strange thing to understand is why these people are contented to live under these conditions. If you're not a black person yourself and if you haven't lived like this, then you simply don'l understand […] They feel safe living segregated from the white community: for the simple reason that they get a secure feeling*

there among themselves. They just haven't got enough confidence in
the white society [...] this is what's wrong with a lot of Aboriginal
people who live like they're living today.

But in Robert Merritt's generation confidence is beginning to grow.
From the freedom rides through the country towns in the 1960s and
the overwhelming vote in 1967 to give the Federal Government charge
of Aboriginal affairs, white awareness of the Aboriginal voice has
been growing. Following that referendum an advisory Council for
Aboriginal Affairs was set up under the chairmanship of Dr. H. C.
Coombs, Governor of the Reserve Bank, and between 1967 and 1972
Federal expenditure on Aboriginal peoples rose from $12,867 a year to
more than $30,000,000. New minds and new sympathies began to be
introduced to matters such as land rights, health and the regeneration of
tribal culture. However, Aboriginal Affairs remained a minor portfolio
without the power to force major changes.

Increasingly vocal black dissatisfaction with the bureaucracy
sought expression on Australia Day, 1972, when black leaders set up
their Aboriginal Embassy in a tent on the lawns of Parliament House.
It remained there for six months until forcibly moved by the police.

It was, however, as a result of such efforts that in 1973, following
a change of Government, a National Aboriginal Consultative Council
was set up by a national black vote to advise the Minister for Aboriginal
Affairs. The Council began with high hopes; but it was a new venture
and in time demonstrated that its constitution needed rethinking. It was
replaced in 1977 with an elected National Aboriginal Conference with
branches in six States and a ten-man executive and an administrative
staff to execute decisions. In a press statement9 on polling day, the
Minister for Aboriginal Affairs, Mr Viner, said that the Conference
would help the Government set long-term goals and priorities in
expenditure. It would also contribute to the evaluation of existing
programmes and the formation of new ones:

The next major step is the assumption by Aboriginals of responsibility
for the success of programmes. This has already been taken at
the local level and the way is open through the bodies now to be
established for a similar step to be taken [...] at a national level.

So, bit by bit, the paternalism and the universal conviction, as Barry Craze put it 'that the Aborigines were a dying race', is passing away; but the problems it left still await resolution. In Paul Coe's words:

> *Even though the Welfare Board has changed its form and its policy, the people who governed blacks under the Welfare Board are the same people who are governing the blacks today. Even if they haven't the legislative power to 'govern', they still have the attitudes to do so, and the economic power to do so.*[10]

Dr H. C. Coombs, one of the sensitive new minds to have worked to find a path of respect and independence for the Australian Aboriginal has demonstrated that to find that respect we must return, humbly, to the beginning of our journey. He tells of an encounter in the West Australian desert with 'a rather broken and derelict group of old chaps' who had reported that nickel mining was destroying their tribe's sacred sites:

> *We set out in a rather broken down old truck, shot a few kangaroos for food and went on to Wingellina. There they took me to the sites, sacred to them and to their ancestors and to see the damage that had been caused […] As the day progressed there was an obvious increase in stature, an increase in authority in these men. Increasingly I became conscious of being a learner, someone who as being instructed in a mystery of infinite complexity […]*
>
> *We went out that night and sat in a circle in the sand with two or three fires between us as they sang the songs of the cycle. They were songs sung in a kind of Gregorian chant […] while they beat the rhythm of the song into the sand with a stick. I sat amongst them, putting my hand on the hand of the man next to me, trying by moving with him to feel the complex rhythm of the song. The night was dark, there was no moon, the only light being from the stars and the fires. For me this was one of the most moving, aesthetic and emotional experiences of my life. In that circle I realised that these people, whom I had presumed to think of as derelicts, had dignity and authority backed by a tradition which ran back through time infinitely beyond that which our own could claim.*[11]

1   *The Wiradjuri Tribe Aborigines on the Lachlan-and their contact with explorers and settlers,* by Barry Craze. Armidale District Historical Society Journal and Proceedings. Editor J. S. Ryan. No. 20, January 1977.

2   George William Evans (1815) John Oxley and Alan Cunningham (1817) James Meehan (1820) and the Land Commissioners of 1839–50 all kept journals or field reports.

3   G.W. Evans, *The Journal of Assistant-Surveyor G. W. Evans on his Expedition to the Lachlan, 1815.* H.R.A. Series 1, Vol. 8, pp 616.

4   *Black Viewpoints, the Aboriginal Experience.* Editor Colin Tatz. ANZ Book Company, Sydney. 1975. p 16.

5   Kevin Gilbert, Senate Select Committee. 1975.

6   *Black Viewpoints,* p l03.

7   In the possession of the Aboriginal Legal Service.

8   *Black Viewpoints,* p 61.

9   *The Weekend Australian,* November 12–13, 1977. National Poll gives Aboriginals 'new voice', by Peter Ward.

10 *Black Viewpoints,* p 103.

11 *This Our Land,* by Stewart Harris, ANU Press 1972, pp 20–21.

Further reading:

Geoffrey Blainey, T*riumph of the Nomads: A History of Ancient Australia.* Macmillan, Melbourne, 1975.

Lorna Lippmann, *Words or Blows: Racial Attitudes in Australia.* Penguin, Melbourne. 1973.

W. H. Stanner, *After the Dreaming.* 1968 Boyer Lectures. Australian Broadcasting Commission Publications.

Top to bottom: Cast in Bondi Pavilion's production of THE CAKE MAN, 1977 (Photo: John Pearson); Teddy Phillips and Brian Syron in ABC TV's production of THE CAKE MAN, 1977 (Photo: John Pearson)

The Cake Man
and the Indigenous Mission Experience

In the introduction to her seminal book *Creating Frames: Contemporary Indigenous Theatre*, Mary Rose Casey observes:

> *Indigenous Australian activists and artist have consistently utilised the potential for theatre [...] to create different frames [...] of Indigenous Australians [...] In a show like* Basically Black *(1972), the ‹gaze› as an expression of racial objectification was returned [...] Following this work, writers such as Robert Merritt, Kevin Gilbert, Gerry Bostock and Jack Davis individually and collectively altered the range of representations of Indigenous Australians in Australian theatres and writing. In doing so, they increased awareness of issues affecting Indigenous people and related those issues to them. as human beings.*

Indigenous Australian culture is the oldest continuous culture on the planet, stretching back many thousands of years. Indigenous engagement with colonially derived theatre is of shorter duration, and it is only in the last fifty years that Indigenous playwrights, in the European sense of that role, have emerged. Robert Merritt, author of *The Cake Man*, is one of this cohort. Written in 1975, his play comes after *Kevin Gilbert's The Cherry Pickers* (1971) but before Jack Davis's *No Sugar* (1985).

The Cake Man is representative of a rich seam of Indigenous playwriting talent, and has a singular, and singularly haunting, nature. On the surface, it is a gentle work, with an elegiac, long-suffering tone reminiscent of Chekhov's dramas of rural stasis. Yet running through the narrative is a wave of political anger and dismay, all the more powerful for being so thoroughly dramatically integrated.

Sweet William, Ruby and Pumpkinhead

The Cake Man is about the mission experience for Indigenous Australians, and the indignity, injustice and often outright exploitation that came from being 'protected' by white Australians with little knowledge and less interest in the traditional culture their arrival near-fatally disrupted.

The play is in three parts. The first section of the first act is a short, symbolic re-enactment of colonial settlement, with an Aboriginal Man, Woman and Child being invaded by a Priest (carrying a bible), a Civilian (carrying a bag of trinkets) and a Soldier (carrying a gun). It introduces the theme of cake that runs throughout the action—the cake that rewards and degrades in equal measure—and the setting for the rest of the story: a rural mission.

The second part of the act is a direct-address monologue by a man who at first glance seems to be the central character. Sweet William is '[an] Australian Aborigine […] made in England', and in a long, inebriated speech he holds forth on his life, wife and days spent knocking on doors 'mak[ing] enquiry, to discover if possible what is it I have that you now want'.

As he talks, Sweet William drinks, and the question of whether alcohol has unmanned him, or being unmanned has led him to alcohol, hovers over the remainder of the play like a dark cloud.

Acts Two and Three show life on the Mission. Ruby, Sweet William's wife, and Pumpkinhead, his young son, live in a fibro shack with the barest of amenities. In a cot is Ruby's new baby, suffering eye sores that have to be regularly washed if they aren't to gum shut her lids. Ruby is a powerful figure. George Ogilvie, who directed the premiere of the play, commented:

> *In rehearsal I had to stress the fact that the role of Sweet William should not be softened with sympathy; because the naturalism of the play is very important. The man's hopelessness is apparent, particularly in the scenes with his wife, who grew […] to become the central focus […] The play deals. with Ruby's problems of a drunken husband and an errant son, and Pumpkinhead's revelation at the end: that his father has finally made a decision. In a sense the father becomes a sacrifice. Pumpkinhead is to be the man who will last the distance.*

Ogilvie is right about *The Cake Man*'s style, which is a beautifully nuanced realism. The dialogue exchanges between the family—the love and loss freighting Sweet William and Ruby's relationship, the anger and need in Sweet William and Pumpkinhead's—are a masterly evocation of mood and locale. The grinding poverty and emotional paralysis of the mission are perfectly rendered, a capturing not so much of the outward detail, as the inner truth, of racial subjugation.

The play breathes with the quality of lived experience, reflecting the fact that Merritt himself grew up on the Erambie Mission at Cowra, and that Pumpkinhead, all elbows and outrage, is a lot like the boy he once was.

Half-Jesus, half-Aboriginal

But there is another dimension to the play, poetic and subtle. It draws its intensity from two sources: Christian imagery and Dreamtime stories. In the minds of Merritt's characters these blend into strange hybrid symbols—and into the tale of the Cake Man; half-Jesus, half-Aboriginal spirit.

Here is Ruby, in the middle of the play, recounting the story to Pumpkinhead, at his request, for the umpteenth time:

RUBY: Long time ago, when Dreamtime's ending, Jesus, he sent the Cake Man over to the sea to find the Kuri children. And he come …

PUMPKINHEAD: With the cake. With the cake Jesus put to carry in his heart. Plenty!

RUBY: He come, with the cake, the cake that was love from Jesus, and he's lookin' 'round then for good children to love and give cake to …

PUMPKINHEAD: Only the bad men stuck a stick in Cake Man's eyes!

RUBY: That's the truth, the bad men, the wicked men done that …

PUMPKINHEAD: And then the Cake Man lose his way, and can't see because his eyes is blind, and he can't see the Kuri boys, only the gubba kids he kin see ever since them bad men done that! Cake Man's a blind man …

RUBY: Yes, and all the time since then, the Cake Man been walkin' around the bush lookin' for somethin' he's forgot about what it was …

PUMPKINHEAD: But he still got all the cakes, and we gotta find him and tell him!

RUBY: He still got all the cakes, that's right, but he don't know any more about who Jesus told him to give 'em to …

PUMPKINHEAD: He forgot! He don't even know he is the Cake Man! His eyes gone blind, and he forgot even who is s'posed to give the cakes to, and he forgot even about havin' to do it. He don' know who he is … gotta tell him!

RUBY: Pumpkinhead, who's tellin this story?

Pause.

Well then, what we got to do, we got still to wait for him, got to keep lookin, till we see him there, and then we tell him about the cakes that Jesus sent to Kuri children, make him know himself, remember he is the Cake Man …

PUMPKINHEAD: Got to stick him in the heart with a spear! Story says that … a spear!

RUBY: Yes, story says that, but I don' know about that part.

PUMPKINHEAD: Yeah! That's the best part, Mum! [*Relishing the idea*] When the Kuri boy finds the Cake Man, then he got stick a spear the Cake Man's heart, right in his heart, and then the Cake Man remembers, and he knows who he is, that he's the Cake Man Jesus sent one time…

RUBY: Well, that's the story … my Daddy told me … yes, it is.

Symbols of integration, separation, belonging and escape recur again and again in Merritt's play, like soft, sombre echoes. Sweet William returns from a half-hearted exercise looking for work, to fall asleep, drunk, in the one chair in the house.

Ruby forgives him, but can he forgive himself? Pumpkinhead won't even look at his father. His fury at the squalid conditions in which they are compelled to live, and Sweet William's inability to do anything about them, irradiates the action.

In the main story, Pumpkinhead has been stealing coal, and this prompts some interaction with the white characters in the play, who are referred to by generic titles: Mission Manager; Inspector; and Civilian. It is from the last that Pumpkinhead has been pilfering fuel to keep warm through the long, bitter, winter nights.

Catching the boy in the act one day, but unable to lay a hand on him, Civilian is incensed, and the darkest moments in the play are the racist diatribes that come of his mouth about the 'blasted lot of delinquent black baby-bushrangers'. Despite the awful content, the writing is never bombastic. It has the ring of truth about it.

Sweet William's search for reality

When the Inspector and Mission Manager bring Civilian to the family's shack, however, the play takes an unexpected turn. Civilian sees Ruby's baby in her cot, and runs away in shock. Next day, when Pumpkinhead goes to return the coal he stole—under Ruby's stern instructions, now she knows where it really comes from—he finds 'a large deep box filled with goodies'.

Civilian appears, and boy and man lug the box back to the Mission, out of which comes a big cake. To Pumpkinhead, Civilian is now the Cake Man, and the stage is suddenly filled with dozens of Indigenous children embracing him and screaming in delight.

It is a stunning reversal and the effect is to complicate the drama without lessening the force of its political message. It is as if the play has expanded, and we are suddenly in a world of larger meaning. Ruby, Sweet William and Pumpkinhead acquire a biblical aura: the Original Family. Civilian—though interestingly, not the Inspector or Mission Manager—becomes capable of regret, remorse and restitution. And if his giving cannot replace what was taken in the first place, it takes the drama to a new spiritual level nevertheless.

Towards the end, Sweet William decides to leave for Sydney. The son can now look at the father with respect, and though Ruby and her husband know that ultimately what awaits him is more degradation (he's unfairly arrested the moment he arrives), the decision is all. Pumpkinhead sees that positive action is possible.

In a theatre culture like ours, with so few Australian dramas from the past revived, *The Cake Man* is more than an historical artefact, a script we read because the chances of seeing it staged are zero-to-non-existent. It is a signpost in the road. The appearance of Merritt's play was apposite and fateful: the year in which the Whitlam government reached a peak of legislative reform, then ran aground on the backroom politics of the Dismissal. Aspiration and frustration were present in equal measure in our national imaginary in 1975. The compelling mood of *The Cake Man* picks up on this divided self and teases it into emotional clarity. Compared to the stentorian denunciatory dramas of Stephen Sewell, Jack Davis, Louis Nowra, and Dorothy Hewett, Merrritt's play is soft and elegiac.

And yet. In the gentle grasp of its authorial vision a human truth is revealed that will fuel Indigenous drama for the next fifty years. The simple-but-profound, humourous-yet-devastating tone of *The Cake Man* can be found in *Stolen, Bran Nue Dae* and *The Sapphires*. As such, it is a permanent addition to the register of our dramatic understanding. And if we can form important thoughts and feelings on our stages, we can form them in our daily lives. These concatenate, shaping the larger realm of public awareness wherein we can act with new purpose to face the country's past and better our lives in the present.

There is a message in *The Cake Man,* certainly. But it is also a message in itself, the re-enactment, in the domain of theatre, of a pain and desire that perhaps lies beyond conscious articulation. Such is the paradox of great playwriting. It puts our experience into words to illuminate experiences that lie beyond words. It opens up a vast sky of imaginative possibility that is inadequately summed up by the term 'legacy'.

I met Robert Merritt shortly before he died. He was a friend of my sister-in-law and came to a dinner she had organised. Time had not been good to him, and his health was poor. I was dimly aware of a grand talent fading away. Re-reading *The Cake Man* years later in the context of an Australia beginning to acknowledge its racist colonial history, I saw it for the remarkable achievement that it truly is: a play born out of violence, oppression and exclusion, that responds to it with love, laughter, mystery and hope.

Julian Meyrick

The Cake Man and the National Black Theatre: Identity through storytelling

The story goes that Bobby Merritt was escorted from prison to see the premiere of his play *The Cake Man* in 1975. This act in itself is a demonstration of the world of the play—on one hand, the world premiere of a groundbreaking work at the only Aboriginal theatre company in the country, juxtaposed with the author still in handcuffs arriving at the theatre in Redfern escorted by police. It is noted that the cast refused to start the performance until Merritt was released from the handcuffs, for the duration of the show at least. By 1975, the National Black Theatre had been engaged for a few years in street theatre and protest performances connected to the Tent Embassy in Canberra and other events throughout Sydney, dedicated to raising awareness and making a political change for Aboriginal and Torres Strait Islander peoples. With very little funding but a sense of purpose, *The Cake Man* emerged—to tell the story of where we had come from, as well as where we are.

Though the 1967 referendum changed the nature of engagement with Government policy makers, it wasn't until late 1972 and the election of the Whitlam Labor Government that we saw material changes for Aboriginal and Torres Strait Islander Australians. With the adoption of the principle of Self Determination, things changed rapidly—the establishment of Aboriginal medical services, housing and legal services, Land Rights policies and education organisation. Alongside this growth of self-determined, community-controlled organisations was the establishment of the National Black Theatre. The thinking was twofold—not just addressing the need for what we now call 'Closing the Gap', but also forms of 'truth telling' and writing onto the public record our stories from our perspective.

From the beginning of the colonial project, the telling of our stories has gone hand in hand with the political advancement of First Nations peoples. Coming from an oral and pictogram tradition, there were limited ways for western scholars to interpret the recorded complex cultural web of story and meaning created over millennia of development of First Nations life on this continent. There are stories from the late-eighteenth century in the early days of the Sydney colony where Arthur Phillip writes of witnessing 'ceremonies' where he was exposed to dances being performed that were warning him off and expressing the aggravated reality of the gathered Eora people.

In the nineteenth century, in what became known as Melbourne (Naarm), William Barak used his painting and song to tell the story of his people. He eventually was instrumental in the petitioning government for the establishment of a homeland community known as Coranderrk. Oodgeroo Noonuccal—in her poem 'Aboriginal Charter of Rights', written in 1962 for the annual conference of FCAATSI (Federal Council for the Advancement of Aborigines and Torres Strait Islanders)—espoused the need for change and demanded equality:

> We want hope, not racialism,
> Brotherhood, not ostracism,
> Black advance, not white ascendance.
> Make us equals, not dependents.

Storytelling continued to be an important device for social change leading up to, and beyond, the 1967 referendum. The birth of the National Black Theatre demonstrates a continuity of performance as political commentary that had been around for centuries. To tell our stories is a political act, even if it is just telling our side of the story, because telling our stories too often feels like we are calling into a void of active forgetting by settler communities who have a vested interest in the persistent narratives of Terra Nullius, a dying race and museum-style anthropology that disallows contemporary experiences.

Robert Merritt, like his unproduced predecessor Kevin Gilbert (who wrote *The Cherry Pickers* in 1968, considered the first written Aboriginal play), found a power in writing biographically and sometimes autobiographically about his experience and the people around him, reflecting the lived experience of being Aboriginal in this country. Those who followed—like Gerry Bostock, Bob Maza, Oodgeroo Noonuccal, Eva Johnson and of course Jack Davis—found an enthusiastic reception for these stories, which showed to a broader audience the power of righting the wrongs of history and steering the national narrative towards a truer representation of First Nations peoples and experiences. Looking back through time, it is hard to imagine a moment when there was such wholesale ignorance of Aboriginal and Torres Strait Islander people and culture, a time when negative stereotypes and colonial perspectives overpowered the truth of the colonial history of this country. Many critics dismiss these early works as didactic or agitprop in their political messaging. However, there is a clear line from the political street theatre and public calls for change that not only informed many of the early works, but also an overwhelming sense of humanity, humour and survival.

The Cake Man has the honour of being the first performed Aboriginal play. It is worthy of note that it was also directed by a First Nations person and commissioned and shepherded through the development process by First Nations people (although Jim McNeil, another playwright incarcerated at Bathurst Gaol around the same time, is credited as assisting Merritt). *The Cake Man* is a symbol of the self determination movement in action. It is worth noting that National Black Theatre found it difficult to receive funding due to their lack of experience at the time and eventually disbanded under the pressure in 1977.

Today there are numerous First Nations companies who receive funding and support, who are commissioning fistfuls of First Nations writers—Ilbijerri established in Melbourne in 1990, Yirri Yaakin established in Perth in 1993 and Moogahlin established in Sydney in 2007. Dance companies, large-scale events, mainstream productions of First Nations plays have become the norm across the country, to the point where it would be difficult for any public entity not to engage in First Nations cultural perspectives. These events, companies and writers owe a huge debt to the early days of National Black Theatre, as it set the tone and purpose for our storytelling that even today continues to inform our national identity—our national storytelling.

Wesley Enoch

The Cake Man was first performed by the Black Theatre at the Black Theatre Arts and Culture Centre, Sydney, on 12 January 1975 with the following cast:

ABORIGINAL WOMAN	Justine Saunders
ABORIGINAL BOY	Teddy Phillips and Lisa Maza
ABORIGINAL MAN	Zac Martin
PRIEST	Dan Adcock
SOLDIER	Rob Steele
CIVILIAN	Max Cullen
RUBY	Justine Saunders
SWEET WILLIAM	Zac Martin
PUMPKINHEAD	Teddy Phillips and Lisa Maza
MISSION MANAGER	Dan Adcock
MISSION INSPECTOR	Rob Steele
MR PETERSON	Max Cullen

Designed by Nick Hollo and Sandy Gray
Directed by Bob Maza

Justine Saunders and Brian Syron in Bondi Pavilion's production of
THE CAKE MAN, *1977 (Photo: John Pearson)*

CHARACTERS

ABORIGINAL WOMAN
ABORIGINAL BOY, aged about eleven
ABORIGINAL MAN
PRIEST
BRITISH SOLDIER of the Colonial period
CIVILIAN, a Colonial squatter
RUBY, an Aboriginal mission woman
PUMPKINHEAD, her son
SWEET WILLIAM, her husband
MISSION MANAGER
MISSION INSPECTOR
MR PETERSON (CIVILIAN), a neighbour

Justine Saunders and Brian Syron in Bondi Pavilion's production of
THE CAKE MAN, *1977 (Photo: John Pearson)*

ACT ONE: GOD AND GUN

A bush scene: a bark humpy, a tree, shrubs, a stream. An ABORIGINAL WOMAN *sits by the humpy working, singing to herself and watching a* BOY, *about eleven years old. The* BOY *is playing with some pebbles, holding about four of them, tossing them up and trying to catch them on the back of his hand. Earth, water, sky: nature at ease.*

The WOMAN *looks off and rises, smiling. The* BOY *pauses in his play and an* ABORIGINAL MAN *strides on, carrying spear and club. He throws two goannas down in front of the* WOMAN. *She picks them up and takes them over to the humpy, expressing her admiration of him. He nods, casual, strong and proud, then lays down his weapons and sits. She fetches him a vessel of water. He takes it from her, nodding, and drinks, then hands the vessel back. She puts it away, embraces him briefly and returns to her chore. The* BOY *approaches the* MAN *from behind while he is drinking, and stands there watching him. The* MAN *turns his head slowly and growls at the* BOY, *who giggles excitedly and runs stealthily behind the humpy. The* WOMAN *stifles a laugh, and the* MAN *grins at her. The* BOY *creeps back, carrying a toy spear and club. He erupts into screeching noise, stamping his feet. The* MAN *spins about, growls and falls to his hands and knees, imitating an animal. They play for some time at hunter and savage beast until the* MAN *grabs the* BOY*'S leg, snapping at it with his teeth, and the* BOY *strikes him in the back with the spear three times. The* MAN *gurgles, collapses and falls in defeat. The* BOY *dances victoriously around the 'body', looking to the* WOMAN *for praise and getting it. When he finishes his dance, the* MAN *sits up. All three embrace. They sit contentedly together, requiring no more.*

Pause.

A kettle drum is heard, off. They sit up stiffly, staring in alarm. Three white men march on, dressed in styles of long ago: a PRIEST, *a* SOLDIER, *a* CIVILIAN. *The* PRIEST *carries a Bible and a long crucifix. The* CIVILIAN *carries a bag slung from his shoulder. The* SOLDIER *carries a musket. The drum noise fades away. The* ABORIGINES *stand quietly to face the white men. The* PRIEST *comes towards them waving a blessing with a hand. The* MAN *pushes the* WOMAN *and* BOY *behind him.*

PRIEST: Greetings! And God's blessing. I bring you good news! Here it is, my child, [*offering the Bible*] for you and your little family. And this also I bring to you [*wagging the cross*] and to your people. The gift of love. The promise of salvation. Yours.

He stands offering the book and the cross. The MAN *stands, shielding his family. Pause.*

You don't understand me! No speakee?

The MAN *shakes a slow head, dumb and proud.*

Oh, come now, take these I say!

The ABORIGINES *move backwards together. The* PRIEST *pauses, turns to his companions.*

He doesn't understand me. [*Shaking his head sorrowfully*] Who would dream, in this age, of such ignorance?

SOLDIER: Well, Father, he must be one of the last. I mean, I've heard it told that God's word has been told the length and breadth of the country. So this lot ought to be about the last lot.

PRIEST: Ah! All our black brothers.

SOLDIER: Aye.

PRIEST: Saved.

SOLDIER: God be praised.

PRIEST: From their ignorance and sin.

SOLDIER: Yes Father, indeed.

PRIEST: And from hell.

SOLDIER: Oh, aye.

PRIEST: Through God's mercy and love.

SOLDIER: Amen.

CIVILIAN: Amen.

PRIEST: I notice, however, that this particular fellow is, ah, well he strikes me as being more of a heathen, poor devil, than most heathens.

SOLDIER: It's as you say, Father, aye.

PRIEST: Very backward indeed. Unfriendly, even.

SOLDIER: Aye, very.

PRIEST: Yes, very very very.

They regard the ABORIGINES *thoughtfully. The* ABORIGINES *regard them fearfully.*

CIVILIAN: Here, I'll reach them with my pretties.

He steps forward, reaching in his bag to bring forth bright beads, ribbons, and so on. He offers them in a coaxing way to the MAN, WOMAN, *and* BOY. *They step back and away from his pretties.*

You refuse? [*Angrily*] Well!

He stuffs the pretties back in his bag. Another pause.

PRIEST: [*sighing*] Well. He refuses, yes.

SOLDIER: Savage ingrate.

PRIEST: Alas, yes. Too ignorant for light, too old for change ...

SOLDIER: Too stupid for words.

PRIEST: Oh, now they are harsh words.

SOLDIER: Well, it's a brute, Father. So it is.

CIVILIAN: No child is a brute, surely?

PRIEST: Exactly not. We must save the child, by all means we must do that. He is, they are, and we all are God's own children, strange as it is, and we must love one another ... or be damned, and lost, and defeated utterly by the power of darkness.

The SOLDIER *hefts his rifle.*

SOLDIER: Never, so long as I live!

PRIEST: Ah! Christian soldier!

The SOLDIER *holds the gun out. The* PRIEST *blesses it briefly.*

SOLDIER: Thank you, Father.

PRIEST: Alas! I have failed.

CIVILIAN: Don't blame yourself, now.

SOLDIER: Aren't the two of us here, Father, both witnesses to your patience?

PRIEST: Bless you, bless you both.

SOLDIER: Aye. Now my duty is plain.

He lifts his rifle ominously.

PRIEST: I must pray!

He falls to his knees, praying, head down. The SOLDIER *shoots the* MAN *dead. The* PRIEST *looks up to see him fall, the* WOMAN *and the* BOY *crying, falling on him in grief.*

Murder! What doest thou? [*Weeping*] Oh, oh, my children! Why killest thou each other? Why murdereth thou each othereth?

The CIVILIAN *is inspecting the corpse.*

[*To the* CIVILIAN] Is it dead? Oh, woe, then, woe to him whose hand obtained the deed! [*Turning to the* SOLDIER] Was I not praying for our answer to this problem? Did you not see me at my prayers? [*Sadly*] Oh, why did you kill this child of God?

SOLDIER: Well, you blessed me rifle.

PRIEST: Thank God for that.

SOLDIER: Anyway there's no law against it.

PRIEST: God's law is against it!

SOLDIER: Well, I wish I hadn't done it.

PRIEST: You confess to the deed?

SOLDIER: To you, Father, aye.

PRIEST: And are you truly sorry?

SOLDIER: Aye. I am indeed.

PRIEST: And was there anything else?

SOLDIER: No, not offhand Father.

PRIEST: Say three Hail Marys, two Our Fathers. And mind, before you go to sleep this night.

SOLDIER: Aye. Thank you, Father.

PRIEST: And remember in the future: heathens they might be, ignorant and superstitious they might also be; but they, as we, are God's own sweet children.

CIVILIAN: Amen.

SOLDIER: Amen.

PRIEST: Yes, and make that six Hail Marys.

SOLDIER: Oh, but Father!

PRIEST: 'Thou shalt not kill.'

CIVILIAN: Amen.

SOLDIER: Oh. Well, all right. Six it must be.

PRIEST: And remember again: your duty is one thing, your immortal soul is another.

SOLDIER: Yes. Well, Amen to that as well.

PRIEST: Worms that we are.

CIVILIAN: Aye.

PRIEST: Weakly flesh. [*Sighing*] Yet not a sparrow falls, remember that, nor does a camel go through the eye of a needle. No jot, or tittle, or anything.

CIVILIAN: Amen.

SOLDIER: Will we bury this one now then?

PRIEST: Yes. Well, first we'll pack up the family, put them in the wagon, prepare them for their journey. [*Smiling*] Ah, yes! And what a journey for them it will be! New life, new love, and a new spirit!

> *The* PRIEST *becomes abruptly businesslike, turning to the grieving but silent* WOMAN *and* BOY *and coaxing them.*

Come, come?

> *They ignore him and sit stonily.*

We must get them in the wagon.

SOLDIER: Leave it to me, Father.

> *He starts a purposeful move.*

PRIEST: No, let me try again. [*Wheedling*] Come? Will you not come now out of darkness into the light? No? [*Shaking his head, smiling sadly*] Oh, you poor savage devils, you don't understand, do you? No, indeed, and how could you know, how could you dream, even, of where you are going—out of your stone-age misery, out, and onwards to every joy of a Christian civilisation, with knowledge, and with comfort and enlightenment … ah, yes!

SOLDIER: Amen!

> *He nods the truth of it at the* ABORIGINES. *They sit grieving and uncomprehending.*

PRIEST: Bring them.

> *He turns and walks a little away.*

SOLDIER: Come on, then! Up! Get you up and to the wagon.

> *He reaches for the* BOY.

Come now!

The BOY *attacks him, sobbing uncomprehendingly with fear.*

So that's it little brute!

He cuffs the child brutally, knocking him down.

CIVILIAN: Oh, stop it now!

He moves quickly to restrain the SOLDIER.

It's not to a child I'll see any of that done. Come away I'll not have that!

SOLDIER: Well, you fetch 'em!

He stands at a distance in bad temper. The BOY *lies hurt and anxious. The* CIVILIAN *tries a smile, reaching out his open arms to the* BOY *and going to pick him up. After a long pause, the* BOY, *watching the promise of kindness in the* CIVILIAN'S *attitude, rises slowly, and slowly reaches up his arms to him. The* SOLDIER *knocks the* CIVILIAN'S *arms down.*

Don't touch it with our own hands! Do you not know of their dirt and how the lice go crawling through their heads, man?

The CIVILIAN *pauses and looks to the* PRIEST.

PRIEST: I should wait till it's washed.

The CIVILIAN *hesitates. He shows every sign of wanting to touch the* BOY *and every sign, too, of fearing the contamination just mentioned. Pause. The* BOY *withdraws.*

We'll try 'em with the old routine. All right now, take up your parts on cue.

The stand apart and cough self-consciously. The PRIEST *winks.*

This'll get 'em for sure!

He claps his hands at the sky and cocks an ear. Music comes from beyond: a piano playing the old Bing Crosby song, 'There's a Happy Land Somewhere'. The PRIEST *sings to the* WOMAN *and* BOY.

Oh, there's a happy land somewhere,
And it's just a prayer awaay.

He carries it through, the others harmonizing.

All you've dreamed and planned is there,
And it's just a prayer awaay!
There'll be good conditions on your friendly Missions
Filled with laughing children at plaay.
Where your hearts will sing for it means one thing
All your old sins will be passed awaay.

They really sing it up.

Ohhhh! There's a happy land somewhere,
And it's just a prayer awaaay.

The music fades away. The PRIEST *stops singing, and holds his arms out wide to the* WOMAN *and* BOY. *They back off in wide-eyed alarm.*

Ohh ... didn't you like that? [*Turning sorrowfully to the other two*] Well, they haven't much ear for music, it seems.

SOLDIER: I thought it was rather good.

They look reproachfully at the ABORIGINES. *The* BOY *stands in front of the* WOMAN, *scowling at the* SOLDIER, *who reacts impatiently.*

Ahhh! [*Going for the* BOY] Come with me now.

There is a struggle involving the SOLDIER, *the* BOY *and the* WOMAN.

CIVILIAN: No!

The SOLDIER *is pulled back. The* CIVILIAN *fossicks in his bag and brings out some cake which he shows to the* BOY, *coaxing him.*

Here, little man, lovely cake. [*Pretending to taste it*] Delicious. Mmmm! Lovely cake.

He backs off, with the BOY *following.*

Ahhh, now that's the clever wee man. Come, I'll give you cake.

The BOY *follows. reaching for the cake, the* WOMAN *following. The* CIVILIAN *coaxes him up to the* PRIEST.

No trouble at all. [*Smiling, offering the cake*] Here it is, then that's a good fellow.

As the BOY *reaches for the cake, the* PRIEST *snatches it away.*

PRIEST: No, mustn't give him that. It would only cause him pain. They are not accustomed to cake, they are not ready for cake.

CIVILIAN: [*confused and angry*] But Father, I promised him the cake.

PRIEST: Oh, promise it by all means.

He eats it. The CIVILIAN *stands back in confusion. The* PRIEST *turns to the* WOMAN *and pushes the bible into her hands. She accepts it dumbly.*

There, take it and keep it always. Keep it, and from it learn wisdom, and faith, and love.

Together with the SOLDIER, *he starts to shepherd the* WOMAN *and the* BOY *off the stage.*

Come ... don't be frightened ... put your trust in us ... we're going to make you our own.

The kettledrum rattles, off. They exit. After a pause, the MAN *opens his eyes and gets groggily to his feet, coughing a little. He discovers a pile of clothes. He picks up a sandshoe and examines it curiously, then another. He tries them out on his hands, then puts them on his feet. He picks up a pair of trousers and experiments with them, trying them on his head and arms before putting them on correctly. A bright red shirt and a cardigan follow. He walks about unsteadily, and it becomes apparent that he is drunk. He looks up and sees the audience for the first time.*

MAN: Uh, who you? [*Grinning craftily*] Hey, listen, you wanna buy a boomerang?

He pulls one from under his coat and holds it up for audience inspection.

Good one, this is. [*Turning it over, reading the back of it*] Made in Japan [*with a grin*] by our trading allies. [*Tossing the boomerang offstage*] There! Now you seen an Abo throw a boomerang. The Australian champeen is a whitefeller now, it's a fact. A Gubba never had a social welfare cheque in his whole life. 'Gubba', that's Kuri lingo for whitefeller. Gubbaahhh, is how y'say it if ever y'overseas tellin' someone. I heerd some people in other places is curious about Kuris, an' about our lingo. I know a bit of it, different words an' that. just ask me an' I'll tell ya.

He poses proudly now.

See'n I'm a Kuri. The Australian Aborigine, that's who I am and what I am ... made in England.

Pause.

Oh! Speakin' of social welfare cheques, y'see that in the paper the other day? [*Ponderously*] The Minister said there is some real evidence to the fact ... that some blackfeller's is spendin' their social on likker. They's buyin' booze. [*With a sigh*] Oh, just like them Red Injuns what ruined 'emselves the same way ... at the firewater all the time. [*Sighing, nodding*] I know it's a fact. Hang on there.

He nicks offstage and returns with a half full flagon of wine. He drinks from it and smiles.

The social cheque came yesterday, thank Christ.

He laughs, drinks, reflects.

Ha, that's what she always says. Rube, my missus, she's always thankin' Christ for everythin' ... anythin' ... nothin'. Her an' that fuckin' book. [*With a laugh*] She heard me say that, I'd be in strife. Christian she is, my old lady, a mission Chrishyun, the worst kind. [*Scratching his head, mock-serious*] What's that bit again? 'For y'travel over land and sea to make one convert ... an' when ya finished with 'im, why, that feller's twice as fit for hell as you are y'self.' [*Laughing gently*] Somethin' like that it goes. In that book of hers. The Jesus rort ... Rort, that's not a Kuri word, it's just Australian. It means that whatever ya got goin' isn't exac'ly the genuine article ... sort of a swindle, y'see.

He pauses, drinks again, then nods.

But I can't say that t'Rube. I did once, I said the Jesus rort was a rort. Whoo, gahd-jeezus! Nearly hit with that book of hers I was, only she frightened to use it like that. [*Chuckling*] She hit me the other time, though. I got drunk again and things are bad and I'm shakin' my fist at the sky like this. [*Demonstrating*] I'm on at her whitefeller God and I'm singin' out at him real loud. 'You dirty Jesus,' I says, 'Come down here, you dirty little Jesus, and I'm gonna give you a drink a my vinegar with me. Ha! you white bastard, you Jew bastard, you gunjie little Jesus ... gunjie bastard ...

He pauses to drink again.

Gunjie is a Kuri word ... means policeman. We say gunjie, it means a white copper animal. Down there at Victoria, now, they got this different word, they say he a berrimaja, the white copper a berrimaja.

He sits down by his flagon.

It's all the same what the words is. Only me, I don't talk much real words to my missus ... have to pretend a thing, have to live it and hide it all the time, anyway I got no strength to put behind what words I say to anyone ... just a fuckin' blackfeller, me.

Pause. He drinks, loses interest for a few seconds, then regards the audience with mild surprise.

You still there? I still got somethin' that you want? What you want from me that I got? [*Leaning forward and coaxing*] Don' be scairt, jus' say it. That's what I wanna know too ...

He stares out dully.

The Australian Aborigine—that's me—stands in danger of losing his identity ... [*Nodding solemnly and drinking*] I read that in an old paper, all about how gubbas is very interested in Dreamtime stories. Uncle Foley's an old blackfeller lives around here and he's about a hunnert years old—he was one of them I been gettin' drunk with t'day, only they gone home now—well, Uncle Foley can tell you them Dreamtime stories. Oh, gahd-jeezus, he knows how everythin' started off once.

Pause. He drinks.

I know one. [*Shyly*] I could tell yuh ... 'bout how the emu lorst 'is wings so can't fly no more. It was on account of this other bird the curlew ...

He stares upwards and recites.

Long time ago the emu had wings and he could fly real fast and he use to show off. The curlew was jealous. One day he came up to the emu and said: 'I betcha I could beat you running.' The big emu looked at the little curlew and laughed: 'You can't beat me at runnin', 'cause I can run just as fast as I fly.' Curlew said: 'We'll just see about that, we'll have a race you and me. What did y'said t'that, Mr. Emu?' Well.

That big flyin' emu said yes. Curlew said: 'Listen, one other little thing is that your wings bein' so much bigger'n my wings, it wouldn't be fair if you was to start flyin' 'stead of runnin'.' Emu said, 'No'. The curlew said: 'We'll both cut our wings.' [*Laughing*] Hhmm, that silly big prick of an emu said all right. [*Chuckling*] 'Come on, we see who's the smartest runner round this claypan. Curlew said give him the knife first and he'd cut off his own wings. So the emu gave the knife to curlew and the curlew went off in the bush with it and pretended to be cuttin' off his wings, all yarmbul-cryin' real loud so the emu would hear and think the curlew was really hurtin' himself cuttin' off his wings ... Yarmbul-cryin', means what y'might call foxin' a bit. Anyway, that curlew went on with his cryin' and yowlin' and makin' a noise ... an'he got a dish of clay—that was filled with blood, and he poured all the blood over his wings and rubbed in some dirt and then he come out again to the emu and give him the knife and said, 'Now it's your turn.' And the silly emu was tryin' to be fair so he took it an' cut off both his own wings straight away there right in front of everybody ... and then he said was curlew ready to race, and the curlew said, 'Yes, let's go,' so they lined up and the race was off—Go!

He pauses and chuckles.

Well, that big emu took off fast as hell, and when he thought he must be far enough in front he peeked back but he couldn't see him anywhere. He heard laughin' and he stopped right there, and he just looked up at the curlew flyin' over the top a him, and he didn't know what to do. [*Drinking again*] Poor old emu, he just put down his head right there, and he sneaked off into the bush ... stayed in there a long time.

Pause.

That's how emu lost his wings.

Pause.

That make any sense, y'reckon?

He shakes his head, wryly.

That Killara Station ... fuck workin' there. [*Smiling*] Social fixed all that anyway. An' wogs. Wogs come in the door, Kuri flies out the window. [*Shrugging*] Probly ain't true, that, but a man's gotta blame things on somethin'. Wogs'll do. They end up buyin' big houses an' runnin' the joint.

He shrugs and sighs. He gestures around.

This is it, here with me mates ... few flagons, then back to the Mission an' bein' Sweet William for me missus. She calls me that, Sweet William. [*Chuckling*] Ain't so sweet, not inside, but no use of lettin' her know what's the inside of the outside of things. If y'know what I mean. I s'pose y'don't ... I'm fuckin' sure I don't.

He drinks.

Most of all I don't know what I got any more that you want. What about a song? Yeah, you like that.

He stands up, prancing, and sings.

> Oh, my girl's a high born lady.
> She's dark but not too shady ...

He pauses and faulters, forgetting the words.

Feather like a peacock ... just as gay ... just as gay ...

He sits down and drinks.

Sorry ... I'm not used to this ... only want to please—to pleasure you all, as my 'Merican cousins'd say. Militant little buggers they are, tch, tch, tch. Nothin' seems to work for them over there ... started off tryin' to please a long time ago too, when the white mens was doin' it to the black womens. Then they changed it round, so the black mens was doin' it to the white womens. What next, I wonder? [*Grinning*] Know what happens when y'cross a black crow with a white rooster? Y'get a magpie. That's why we got so bloody many magpies in Australia and parts elsewhere.

He pauses and drinks.

Uncle Foley's grandfather was Irish. He didn't stay but returned to his estate over there. He was what they call a black Irishman, borne out by the fact that his grandson, Uncle Foley, is also black ... black ... black-black-black! That was my famous imitation of an Aboriginal duck—black-black-black.

He grows silent, then stern. He drinks. Pause.

I suppose this shits you as much as it does me?

He stands.

Look, actually I'm here to make an enquiry, to discover if possible what it is I have that you now want. [*Whining*] Please, boss, you bin tell 'im Jacky, then him plurry happy! What is it?

Pause. He stands in appeal.

No? Well, there y'are. Me boomerang won't come back.

He drinks again, now awfully drunk.

Well, I'm as sick of this as you are. [*Sighing*] … I thought I might be able to say somethin' … not to no gubbas what wear uniforms of any kind, but come along here an' had a yarn. We might of got together and made a magpie.

Pause.

Nothin' wrong with magpies, not really. But it has to be black one part an' white another part so it makes one whole bird. It's hard t' 'splain.

If you'll sit there a bit longer [*picking up his flagon*] I'll try show y' somethin'.

He exits with his flagon staggering. The next act begins immediately.

ACT TWO: THE HAPPY LAND

SCENE ONE

Inside a house on a mission for Aborigines, it is night. The walls are wooden below, fibro on top. A wood stove with a pot and a billy on it, hardly any fire in it and no fuel in sight; cupboards; a table; a battered leather armchair with a Bible lying on it; a baby's cot; an upside-down kerosene tin and an upturned box by the table—no sign of normal kitchen chairs.

RUBY, *the woman from Act One, now 'civilised', stands using a flat iron over brown paper to iron a child's shirt dry. Three candles in old sauce bottles provide her light. She sighs, looks at the iron and spits on it, then goes and puts the iron on top of the stove, but a glance into the fire box disappoints her. She goes back to the table, picks up short pants and a school jumper, folds them neatly and lays them aside. She is careworn, greying and sad.* PUMPKINHEAD, *the* BOY, *also 'civilised', sits playing on a blanket on the floor, tossing some pebbles and catching them on the back of his hand. In the cot a baby starts crying.*

RUBY: Oh, that's Bubby, Pumpkinhead. You be my good boy and see him a minute, while I'm doin' your school clothes dry for tomorrow?

PUMPKINHEAD: Yeah, I get Bubby, Mum.

He goes to the cot, looks in and reaches a gentle hand to do something with the baby.

He got his eyes stuck again, Mum. Sores is stickin' 'em all shut. Can' open 'em.

RUBY: [*anguished*] Oh!

Wringing a cloth in a bowl of water.

Look here, do it with this, good boy, do it soft.

She throws the cloth. PUMPKINHEAD *catches it and turns to reach into the cot, gently wiping the baby's eyes.*

PUMPKINHEAD: Hey, I'm fixin' you, Bubby. No cryin'.

The crying ceases.

RUBY: Oh, you're my good boy.

She retrieves the iron and quickly finishes the. shirt, frowning at the iron. PUMPKINHEAD *returns to his blanket and pebbles.*

Oh, dear, ain't enough fire in the stove to make it hot enough. Be lucky you get your stuff done for school.

PUMPKINHEAD: [*rising again*] Be orright, Mum. Don' care I can't go to school.

RUBY: Pumpkinhead, love, you be a good boy and go see for some coal, maybe a little piece, a bit of wood maybe, to make some little bit of fire?

PUMPKINHEAD: Ain't no coal, Mum, no wood, nothin'.

RUBY: Maybe you find some chips then, good boy?

PUMPKINHEAD: It's dark. Get you coal tomorrow, Mum.

RUBY: Mum'll stand right at the door.

PUMPKINHEAD: No, birriks might get me. Sweet William said, birriks get me I go out in the dark.

RUBY: You don' call your father Sweet William.

PUMPKINHEAD: Birriks.

He jibs obstinately, afraid.

RUBY: Listen, you think you get out of school 'cause no hot iron, boy, you got another think comin'. Now come on, I stand at the door, talk to you all the time while you try find me some chips. Pumpkinhead …

PUMPKINHEAD: I ain't goin' no school I ain' got no dinner. Gubbas look at you. Eat their cakes and make me see 'em when they know I ain't got nothin' … no dinner.

Pause.

RUBY: [*pained*] You know what the Welfare said.

PUMPKINHEAD: Don' care.

RUBY: You don' care—I care! Welfare said you miss any more school they put you in the home for bad boys.

PUMPKINHEAD: Don' care.

RUBY: They do that to my baby I'll die. [*Coaxing*] Oh, Pumpkinhead. Come on, you find Mum some chips.

PUMPKINHEAD: Mum, there ain't no chips out there. The birriks is out there, can' go out there.

RUBY: [*sighing*] Oh, I'm a poor woman.

PUMPKINHEAD: Ain't goin'.

Pause.

Gubbas ain't gonna send me to no home. I'll run away in the bush, I will, when they try and get me for the home.

RUBY: They just catch you again ... take you.

PUMPKINHEAD: No. I'll get a spear stick it in 'em. Then when I come back I'll take you and Bubby down to big Sydney and buy a big red house and have a TV and Bubby can take sandwiches and cakes to school for his dinner and gubbas can't look at him.

He frowns, dreaming defiantly. She goes and puts her arms around him.

RUBY: Son, you're my good boy, but can't run away in the bush, can't figure things with no spears.

PUMPKINHEAD: I'll be a bushranger.

RUBY: They hang you sure then.

But she smiles and rubs his head. Then she goes to put away the clothes, hanging the shirt for drying.

PUMPKINHEAD: I get you some bits of coal, Mum, where I get it from the railway. Tomorrow after school, if I go to school, get the coal any rate.

RUBY: You careful on that railway line. I'm happy for the coal you find there, good boy, but won' be happy you're not careful and train get you.

PUMPKINHEAD: Not when I'm gettin' coal, no train get me.

RUBY: Oh that's good then. Now there's all your wearin' for school tomorrow. All clean again. Soon be time for your bed, gettin' late like it is.

PUMPKINHEAD: Um. Pub shut soon. Sweet William comin' home.

RUBY: Don' call your father that, I tol' you!

PUMPKINHEAD: Your husban' be home soon then.

RUBY: [*angrily*] You call your father your father. [*More angrily as he ignores her*] You hear me, you cheeky little bugger. Now see you made me swear, and all because you damn hatin' your good man father who loves you. Your good man father, you hear me say that, Pumpkinhead?

He stands obstinate, pressing his lips tightly together and starting to breathe emotionally. She sees his tears coming.

Oh, now why you gonna cry? Ain't you my big boy? My good brave boy what's maybe a bushranger soon?

She goes to embrace him. He pulls away, trying to defeat his own tears. But as she stands helplessly he starts to sob with great heaves, turning away with his back to her, then sobbing more and more. Pause. Watching him, she reaches gently with a hand, and the BOY *suddenly turns to bury his face in her and hold on to her with his hands, crying into her.*

There ... I know ... your Ruby understands, yes she does ... my good boy ... there ...

She strokes him, his shoulders, his hair, and he starts to subside. She leads him to the armchair, and sits down. He slides down to the floor, with his body against her knees and his head leaning close.

All right, now come on, we'll have a nice story before our bedtime comes. Nearly time now, we have a Jesus story to get happy, hey?

He sniffs. He recovers. He raises his face to her.

PUMPKINHEAD: Cake Man. I like the Cake Man.

RUBY: [*jollying him, smiling*] Oh, the Cake Man! We'll tell about the Cake Man, will we?

He looks up, nods, trying a smile.

Well come on, you gotta laugh first!

She reaches suddenly to prod and tickle him. They wrangle a second, then he giggles and is recovered.

There! You my funny man again!

PUMPKINHEAD *smiles, and waits.* RUBY *settles herself a hand on his head, stroking, and there begins a story session in which* PUMPKINHEAD *becomes altogether involved, forgetting his worries.*

Ready, now see if I remember. You have to help me. [*Beginning*] Long time ago, when Dreamtime's ending, Jesus, he sent the Cake Man over the sea to find the Kuri children. And he come ...

PUMPKINHEAD: With the cake. With the cake Jesus put to carry in his heart. Plenty!

RUBY: He come, with the cake, the cake that was love from Jesus, and he's lookin' round then for good children to love and give cake to …

PUMPKINHEAD: Only the bad men stuck a stick in Cake Man's eyes!

RUBY: That's the truth, the bad men, the wicked men done that …

PUMPKINHEAD: And then the Cake Man lose his way, and can't see because his eyes is blind, and he can't see the Kuri boys, only the gubba kids he kin see ever since them bad men done that! Cake Man's a blind man …

RUBY: Yes, and all the time since then, the Cake Man been walkin' around the bush lookin for somethin' he's forgot about what it was …

PUMPKINHEAD: But he still got all the cakes, and we gotta find him and tell him!

RUBY: He still got all the cakes, that's right, but he don't know any more about who told him to give 'em to …

PUMPKINHEAD: He forgot! He don't even know he is the Cake Man! His eyes gone blind, and he forgot even who he s'posed to give the cakes to, and he forgot even about havin to do it. He don' know who he is … gotta tell him!

RUBY: Pumpkinhead, who's tellin' this story?

Pause.

Well then, what we got to do, we got still to wait for him, got to keep lookin' till we see him there, and then we tell him about the cakes that Jesus sent to Kuri children, make him know himself, remember he is the Cake Man …

PUMPKINHEAD: Got to stick him in the heart with a spear! Story says that … a spear!

RUBY: Yes, story says that, but I don' know about that part.

PUMPKINHEAD: Yeah! That's the best part, Mum! [*Relishing the idea*] When the Kuri boy finds the Cake Man, then he got to stick a spear in the Cake Man's heart, right in his heart, and then the Cake Man remembers, and he knows who he is, that he's the Cake Man Jesus sent one time …

RUBY: Well, that's the story … my daddy told me … yes it is.

Pause. They sit quietly. She strokes his hair. PUMPKINHEAD *sighs and looks up at her.]*

PUMPKINHEAD: Arr, ain't no Cake Man, Mum.

RUBY: There is so too! [*Pretending to be cross*] Now you stop that, little Pumpkinhead, there is so.

PUMPKINHEAD: No, there ain't.

RUBY: [*firmly*] Ain't no birriks, is what there ain't. You sayin' believe in silly ghosts but no Cake Man?

PUMPKINHEAD: Gubba kids said there ain't. They tol' me and Collie and Noelie and Collie's Sissy …

RUBY: Gubba kids! How they know, them kids?

PUMPKINHEAD: No Father Christmas, they know that. They knows, 'cause they's gubba. That Ralphie knows.

RUBY: I ask you how? Gubba kid just a kid, same as you are and Collie and Noelie.

PUMPKINHEAD: Ralphie knows. He said you buy toys from the shop and when mothers got no money ain't no Santa gonna come to no Kuri kids.

RUBY: Oh!

PUMPKINHEAD: An' I seen the money name tickets on all the toys too, I have, and me and Bubby ain' got no toys, so that's why no Father Christmas … only got birriks I can see.

RUBY: You fibber! Can't see no birriks either! Where you seen birriks, you bugger of a boy?

PUMPKINHEAD: Seen 'em. Me and Collie and Noelie seen 'em. Two of 'em all dressed in black down the church and we were scairt and we run all the way to the mission and we told Uncle Foley and he said they was so! He said they holy birriks and he knows 'cause he's wise!

RUBY: Uncle Foley! That liar ol' man! [*Softening*] Oh, now don' you listen to no gubba kids or no silly old men. [*Reassuring*] Your Ruby tellin' you there sure is a Cake Man. Jus gotta find the feller.

PUMPKINHEAD: We all been lookin' to find him. We been lookin' all in the bush, everywhere, and we been up the streets in the town, lookin' to see the man who can't see us. [*Sighing*] But they see us.

Pause.

RUBY: No, they don' see you.

PUMPKINHEAD: Huh! They chase me and kick my arse damn good for no seein' me.

RUBY: You wash your mouth.

She hits him a light slap on the head.

PUMPKINHEAD: [*hushing her suddenly*] Listen.

They cock their heads, listening. A dog starts to bark outside We hear, getting louder, the sound of a man singing.

WILLIAM: Ohhhh, Ned Kelly was born in a ramshackle hut,
He battled since he was a kid.
He grew up with bad men and duffers and thieves,
And learned all the things that they did.

He breaks off, cursing the dog. The barking stops. Pause.

SWEET WILLIAM, *the man from Part One, enters, resuming his song.*

Oh, Ned Kelly was born with duffers and— [*Nodding drunkenly as he closes the door behind him*] Ah, you sittin' up late, Rube?

He stands swaying.

RUBY: You see, Sweet William. I got some nice tucker on that stove.

She pulls the upturned kerosene tin over to the stove, gently pushing him to sit down. He sits and looks drunkenly at PUMPKINHEAD, *who looks at him sullenly and turns away.*

WILLIAM *opens his mouth to speak to* PUMPKINHEAD, *then sighs and hangs his head tiredly.* RUBY *takes an enamel dish and tips a little vegetable food from a pot. She gives the dish and a spoon to* WILLIAM. *He eats slowly. The baby cries in its cot.* WILLIAM *stands, muttering with concern. He puts his plate on the floor and heads for the baby.* PUMPKINHEAD *shoves at him bitterly.]*

PUMPKINHEAD: Git away. I do that.

WILLIAM *stands drunk, hurt, and uncertain. Then he stumbles back to his tin and plate, sitting dejectedly and staring down.* PUMPKINHEAD *wets the cloth. He goes to the cot and repeats his performance of bathing the baby's eyes. The crying stops.* RUBY *looks on reasonably. She goes to sit in her armchair, stroking the Bible.*

RUBY: Pumpkinhead.'

He looks to her form the cot.

You're my good boy.

He smiles at her sadly and attends the baby.

Time for your bed now.

She regards PUMPKINHEAD *and* SWEET WILLIAM *anxiously.*

PUMPKINHEAD: I know, Mum.

He concentrates on the baby. WILLIAM *drops the plate and spoon. He starts to talk in a dull tone, not looking at either of them.*

WILLIAM: Ahhhh, you're a good woman, Rube, too good for me. [*Laughing dully*] Sweet bloody William, they call me, huh, the jacky with the 'baccy … 'n' the wine. Ha, cigarceeects 'n' whisky.

He pauses tiredly. RUBY *fidgets anxiously and looks to* PUMPKINHEAD.

RUBY: Bubby's good now, good boy. Come on, it's time for your bedtime. You go now, Mum'll come in in a minute.

She gestures to the bedroom door. PUMPKINHEAD *nods, goes slowly to stand by her, and touches her as she touches him, both miserable.*

WILLIAM: [*shaking his head*] That's what I'll do. That's the place. Nobody cares what colour, long as he works. Can work any gubba in the ground any damn day, done it before today..

He muses. RUBY *carries the cot off to the bedroom. She comes back to* PUMPKINHEAD. *She stands quietly, regarding* WILLIAM, *then gently pushes* PUMPKINHEAD *before her and they go into the bedroom, taking a candle.* WILLIAM *sits alone, muttering to himself.*

Arr, yeah Rube … [*Nodding, affirming it to himself*] Used to do it, till they went 'n brung them Balt bastards in—. bastards. [*Explaining*] Not that I got nothin' personal 'gainst no-one.

Pause. RUBY *comes back and looks at him sadly.*

That's it, Rube. Bring the light back.

She puts the candle down. She goes slowly to sit in her old chair. She sits stroking the book, and opens it during his next lines.

But a man's got nothin' not even the little bit used to be there. Got to get a quid, same as anybody. Arr, but Jesus, [Sighing] I mean there used to be a bit of a go once. Damn it Rube, those bloody Balts the ones that took it all.

Pause. RUBY *looks at him. She shakes her head and sighs, then reads quietly again.*

The fruit season, they were the good old days. Man could go to town them days, hold his head up, Rube. [*Thinking* PUMPKINHEAD *is still there*] Y'hear that, do ya, Pumpkinhead—Your ol' man used to hold up his head them days. Jist ask your mother.

RUBY *starts to look emotional at his words.*

He focuses on her again, catching her eyes. She nods gently, agreeing with him. He loses focus again. He talks at his feet.

But there's work still down the city. [*As something appeals he starts chuckling*] Hah, hah! Sydney's the place! Got their own bloody pub, the Kuris have … [*Amazed*] fancy that. Man can stand up at the bar and have a good go. [*Living it*] Hey, your shout, mate! Sweet William, it's your bloody shout! [*Grinning*] And with your own damn money, too, that y'earned all by yourself.

He falls silent. She reads on, the same page, glancing at him once or twice as he sits starting to sway on the tin.

He falls to the floor and lies there like an old rag. She sighs. She puts her Bible down and goes to raise him up, pulling as he climbs to his feet.

RUBY: Now just you easy, my Sweet William.

She leads him to her armchair and sits him in it. He slumps. She pulls the ironing blanket off the table and throws it over him. She stands sadly. Gradually growing louder, until the curtain. We hear Janis Joplin singing 'Mercedes Benz'. She pushes the pots and billy off the stove. She blows out one candle and fusses about. She picks up the other candle, carries it to the door, where she pauses, looking sadly at SWEET WILLIAM. *She blows out the candle. In the dark, Janis Joplin ending song: 'Oh, Lord, won't you buy me a Mercedes Benz'.*

SCENE TWO

Next afternoon. The backyard of a house: clothes line; various bits of junk lying about; a fairly high fence with a gate shut with an inside bolt; a wood box; a coal bin.

The CIVILIAN, *dressed in modern work clothes, is pottering about in the yard. There is a noise at the gate. He hears it and backs off, quietly waiting. A small black hand comes through the gate and fiddles to open the bolt. The* CIVILIAN *hides. The gate opens and* PUMPKINHEAD *enters stealthily, dressed neatly in school jumper, with his socks pulled up. Quickly and quietly he goes straight to the coal bin, plucks five or six lumps of coal and shoves them inside his shirtfront. As he turns to leave, the* CIVILIAN *JUMPS out of hiding.*

CIVILIAN: Gotch!

He blocks PUMPKINHEAD'*s exit then advances on him slowly.*

Right, now put back my property.

PUMPKINHEAD *looks about, hesitating. The* CIVILIAN *gestures abruptly.*

Go on, you little spook bastard!

PUMPKINHEAD *turns, defeated, reaches in his shirt to pull out a piece of coal. He hesitates.*

Go on, go on you little swine. Put it all back. [*Nodding in nasty satisfaction*] Got you this time, haven't I?

PUMPKINHEAD *makes as if to throw the piece of coal back in the bin, but instead he suddenly lobs it over the* CIVILIAN'*s head.*

Whaaa?

He dodges, and tries to catch the lump of coal. PUMPKINHEAD *reaches swiftly to grab another lump, dodges around him and flies from the scene. The* CIVILIAN *chases him with a shout of anger and dismay.*

You sneaky—! Come back here! Come back with my property! Black bastard! Mission rat!

He halts at the empty gate. The bird has flown altogether.

Right, well that's it. I'll just get my coat on, and we'll see about you thieving lot of dirty …

He mutters and glares out the gate. Then stomps resolutely off.

SCENE THREE

The same afternoon. The house on the mission. RUBY *is sitting in her chair, reading her Bible. The door opens and* SWEET WILLIAM *comes in. He looks at* RUBY, *gets a smile, sighs and goes to sit by the stove.*

WILLIAM: Huh. You prain' again, Rube?

RUBY: Now don't you go talkin' like that, Sweet William. That's why we never have no luck all the time. Do you good, it would, to read this book, that's where I get my strength from in every day, truly is.

WILLIAM: Couldn' do me no more good than a smoke would right now, Rube. Or a little drink.

RUBY: Don't want you talkin' like that in the presence of this here good book, Sweet William!

WILLIAM: Huh! [*Reaching*] Give it here then, Rube, and I'll get me strength back. [*Grin and sigh*] I been all over the bloody mission, haven' I, tryin' to get a draw, an' I'm plain buggered.

RUBY: You're a sad man, Sweet William.

She gets up and takes the Bible to the bedroom.

WILLIAM: Humph. I say I am.

He gets up and starts to wander about the room.

I don' know, Rube, buggered if I do. Man's been all around, everywhere … nothin' bloody doin'.

RUBY: [*off*] You try your Uncle Foley?

WILLIAM: Course I did. First. Thought I'd be a sure thing. 'Specially I said it was for you.

RUBY: [*entering*] You damn devil of a man. Shouldn't do that, sayin' things is for me.

WILLIAM: [*wryly*] I know it. Old bastard give me a lecture, that's all, 'bout bringin' your nerves on again.

RUBY: He give you a smoke?

WILLIAM: Uh. Said he smoked his last bumper this mornin'.

RUBY: Oh. What else he say?

WILLIAM: Nothin'. Oh, yeah, he said give you this.

He fishes out a small paper packet.

RUBY: [*opening it*] Tea!

She smells it, smiling.

WILLIAM: Yeah, I know, just what you need.

RUBY: Just what I need.

WILLIAM: That's what I said.

RUBY: [*delighted*] Start right now!

She grabs the billy off the stove and leaves the room. SWEET WILLIAM *prowls about muttering aloud.*

WILLIAM: Old bastard … can't mind his own business … tellin' me I should pack up and get out of this damn stinkin' place. Go to Sydney, get work, get a decent place for Ruby and the kids. All you need is spirit, just put your shoulders back, take a good job and get some good money, bring Rube and the kids to a—ah, damn shit! Sydney!

He paces slowly in peevish thought.

All right for Uncle Foley, old bastard, he ready for his grave with nothin' to care about no more. [*Scoffing*] Him and his shit talk about the Dreamtime.

RUBY: [*coming back, putting the billy on the stove*] What you sayin' to yourself, Sweet William?

WILLIAM: Ah, nothin' … nothin' Rube.

RUBY: You never mind. Feel better when I make this nice tea. We'll have it, you and me.

WILLIAM: How would I get to Sydney!

RUBY: What's that?

He shakes his head and sits down. She shakes hers and goes to the cupboard. She takes out two Golden Syrup tins, puts them on the table, then goes to stir the fire in the stove, adjusting the billy.

RUBY: Get you nice tin of tea.

WILLIAM: You good, Rube.

He sighs and looks at the floor. She looks at him, fond and sad.
She goes behind him and starts to massage the back of his neck.
He sighs and relaxes gratefully.

RUBY: Never you mind, Sweet William.

WILLIAM: Ah, Rube. [*Miserably*] Ain't nothin' but to mind … your Sweet William ain't so sweet, just what they say, he's a no-good nigger.

RUBY: No he is not.

WILLIAM: Why not, Rube?

RUBY: Well … niggers is Americans.

WILLIAM: Ah.

RUBY: My William ain't no 'Merican.

WILLIAM: No, but he ain't no use either, Rube.

RUBY: Oh, never mind. You don't worry with me. I know what's your fault and what isn't. I know how you're feelin'. I know you tried a long time.

WILLIAM: Oh, yeah, Rube … [*Sighing, enjoying his massage*] But, Rube, there ain't nothin' now I know to do. Just hopeless, and no price I can pay because there ain't no price I've got to give that anyone wants. I got nothin' they want!

RUBY: Got to have faith. That's what God wants.

WILLIAM: God wants!

RUBY: Sit still. Something will turn up, I know.

WILLIAM: Even Pumpkinhead, even my own son hates me. He blames me for all this. And it's not my fault, it isn't, Rube, you know it ain't my fault. You know I'd give my right arm—If there's a God he can have my right arm if he'll let me give you and the kids everything and make Pumpkinhead proud of me. [*Sighing*] But he ain't proud of me like this … I wouldn't want him to be.

RUBY: He will, Sweet William. He's only eleven, one day when he understands … be proud of you then.

WILLIAM: If he could just know what it does to me, when I have to beg … when I don't want to.

RUBY: Well … you wait, one day when our boy Pumpkinhead looks back on life, then you just see how he knows who was the man and he'll have the right one who's his father … yes.

Pause.

WILLIAM: Make the tea, then, Rube. And I'll go into town ... see if I can get ... what I can get.

RUBY: You mean credit?

WILLIAM: I said try, Rube.

She smiles, stops the massage, strokes his hair, then moves away to the billy.

RUBY: Can't do no more than try, Sweet William.

WILLIAM: Trouble is, Rube, credit is hard.

RUBY: [*busy at the stove*] Mmmmnnn?

WILLIAM: All the shops, they know me.

RUBY: Oh.

WILLIAM: It's wrong, it's back to front, Rube, see? Credit's supposed to be when you come from their town and they know you.

RUBY: [*looking at the water*] It won't be long.

WILLIAM: Uncle Foley, he says I should go down to the city, and make something and take you and the kids after me when I done it.

RUBY: That's for you to think, not Uncle Foley.

WILLIAM: He says nothin' here in Cowra, never will be, nothin' but the Mission and like this.

RUBY: Sydney is a long way, Sweet William.

WILLIAM: Henry, he walked there.

RUBY: Well, you ain't got no train fare neither.

WILLIAM: Can walk as good as Henry.

RUBY: [*smiling*] To Sydney? Why, Sweet William, that Henry already had brothers and sisters waitin' for him in Sydney when he got there. Different for you, and where would you go even when you got there.

WILLIAM: I know where I'd go.

RUBY: Where then?

Pause.

I ask you where?

WILLIAM: There's a place ... I know.

RUBY: And I know what you know, Sweet William! You thinkin' of that dirty pub! That low-life, no-good stinkin' pub in that Sydney where all stupid country boys go when they get there 'cause they don't know anywhere else to go and then they get nothin' but mad with

the booze in 'em and no work and no money and in the gaol before
they knows where they are!

WILLIAM: All the brothers and sisters go there, Rube, even Uncle Foley
said that to me. He did, today, you just ask him. He says if a cousin
come there from the bush, why, they gonna help him along and see
him right pretty soon ...

RUBY: How they see him right? How? What they've got to see him
right with? [*Lecturing knowledgeably*] I tell you, Sweet William,
they ain't all stayin' in that pub 'cause they want togetherness, now!
Oh, no, they all there because them white people don' allow no
black people to drink any other place! That's why!

WILLIAM: You been there, Rube?

RUBY: You don't be smart with the questions, Sweet William. I don't
have to been there, it's everybody knows about that dirty pub ...
it's everybody knows that they don't nothin' but get drunk and go
to the gaol.

> WILLIAM *nods and sighs,* RUBY *shakes the tea into the billy.*

Now we just let that stew a minute.

WILLIAM: I been stewin' all my life. Ain't made me no better, Rube.

> *He grins.*

RUBY: You always tasted good to me.

> *They smile at each other.*

WILLIAM: I'm goin' sour now, though, Rube. Time's gettin' along, and
I ain't got nowhere, ain't got you the things we used to plan on.
I don't get a leg on, Rube, gonna be too late.

RUBY: Never too late, Sweet William.

> *She brings the billy, holding it with a cloth in one hand, and*
> *pours tea into the tins.*

We just got to trust in God, don't I keep tellin' you? And you see
how good it comes one day.

> *She returns the billy to the stove; she picks up the old flat iron*
> *and puts it on to get hot; she goes to sit with William and drink*
> *some tea.*

WILLIAM: You puttin' the iron on early, Rube?

RUBY: Got to wash the clothes for school and iron 'em dry. Must be gettin' now, send late for the bread ration, don't let me forget … got some spinach they not gonna want for their tea.

WILLIAM: Rube, I'll just go down to that Sydney, I'm gonna be lucky and get a job and find somewhere that's gonna be ours, and soon buy a big red house like Pumpkinhead wants and clothes and a 'lectric iron for you, 'lectric light, too, and plenty of tucker for the kids that we could buy out of my good job I'll get. I can work, Rube, you know I can. Job, that's all it needs.

RUBY: [*pausing*] You keep sayin' it a lot today … makin' me think you might be meanin' it.

WILLIAM: I am meanin' it, Rube. I got to try.

RUBY: Sweet William, you have to think about what you want … got to decide, and you don't ask no woman of yours what you gonna do, but you can tell me what you gonna do and I'll know that's right and you gotta do it and I know you will too.

WILLIAM: You really think that, Rube? You do?

RUBY: I tell you so.

WILLIAM: Ah, Rube, you tell me so. [*Wryly*] But you don't tell me what you know, about how you feel, I never heard you tell the truth about me yet.

RUBY: Yes you just did.

WILLIAM: I just heard you tell what a good woman you are, Rube … pretendin' I'm not no good.

  Pause.

RUBY: You sayin' I told a lie, Sweet William?

WILLIAM: Just a white lie. But I know, Rube.

RUBY: How do you know what I think, huh?

WILLIAM: Just been married to you for years, Rube. [*Smiling*] I know you say things.

RUBY: You know my good book, Sweet William?

WILLIAM: Not as good as you do, Rube.

RUBY: Well I swear on my good book, that's what I do. I swear what I said is sort of true.

WILLIAM: Rube, I'm sick of hearin' you tell the kids damn stories that ain't never comin' true. All about Jesus loves us, and how one day we're gonna find the Cake Man …

RUBY: Jesus is true. Cake Man is true. Shut up.

WILLIAM: Ah, Rube … ain't no Jesus ain't no man who … They just stories.

RUBY: Shut your wicked mouth, Sweet William!

WILLIAM: Sick of it, Rube, tired of knowin' that Pumpkinhead makes me tell him stories too. You know that, Rube, about the bushrangers, about Jimmy Governor, how the Kuris used to be brave, and how we'd fight and run and fight again …

RUBY: What's wrong with you, you stupid man? You forgot what you liked when you was a little boy? You don't want your own boys to have some stories from their own father? They got no 'spensive books like the gubba boys got, no-one but you and me to have stories for 'em … and you too tired?

WILLIAM: Rube, will you stop pretendin'?

RUBY: What you're sayin', you fool of a man?

WILLIAM: Pumpkinhead … he don't want no stories about the Kuri bushrangers … not 'cause he likes me tellin' him stories, Rube. No, that boy he makes me tell about when the Kuris were brave, and he's only meanin' to make me know about myself.

RUBY: What?

WILLIAM: You know what, Rube … about me, I ain't never stuck up no white man, and I ain't done not one thing in my whole life is brave. All my life, all I ever done was be a jacky-boy.

RUBY: You done your best!

WILLIAM: And my son wouldn't spit on me.

RUBY: He would so!

WILLIAM: [*laughing sadly*] He would damn so. I know.

RUBY: He's only eleven, a baby boy.

WILLIAM: He looks at me sometimes, I get the feelin' our baby boy is a hundred years old.

RUBY: I don' know this fool talk.

WILLIAM: I'll go to Sydney, Rube, and I'll make everything right before it's too late. Right now, tomorrow, and I'll make good

> SWEET WILLIAM *waits for* RUBY *to answer.* RUBY *goes slowly to get herself more tea.*

RUBY: Some more tea, Sweet William?

WILLIAM: No, you keep it, Rube.

She comes back and sits down. WILLIAM *avoids her eyes.*

RUBY: What you say is good, Sweet William.

WILLIAM: [*encouraged*] You think so Rube?

She nods.

I tell you what, I go down there to that city. I'm gonna do like Uncle Foley said, get me some spirit, hold my head up with my shoulders back. You won't hear from nobody that they ever seen me drunk like you been used to.

RUBY: That's happy talk you're sayin'.

WILLIAM: A good job. Rube, you know I'll get us that red house, in just a little while down there.

RUBY: Well, I'll ... be watin' for it.

WILLIAM: You believe that? Me?

RUBY: I believe.

WILLIAM: That I won't get drunk?

RUBY: Course.

WILLIAM: And the red house?

RUBY: I'm plannin' the furniture.

WILLIAM: Why you believe me?

RUBY: Well, I been lovin' you a long time, Sweet William, don't you know that already?

WILLIAM: I mean it, Rube ...

RUBY: So do I ... and we'll be waitin' here.

The baby starts crying in the cot.

Oh, Bubby.

She goes to the cot, reaching a hand in gently, then turns and goes swiftly for a cloth, dipping it in some water, visibly upset as she talks.

Oh, Will, his eyes are stuck shut again.

She reaches in to bathe the baby's eyes gently, crooning to the child, and it stops its noise.

He sleeps all the time, and when he sleeps the sores run. Then his eyes get stuck.

WILLIAM: [*hovering near her*] Can I do somethin', Rube?

RUBY: No, I'm used to it. Haven't I had it with both of them? Just have to clean it away all the time. [*Beseeching him*] Do you mean it, Will? You'll go, and you won't get drunk, and you'll get us out of here ... William?

WILLIAM: I mean it, Rube ... you'll see, you wait.

> *He goes to her and holds her gently. She puts her arms around him, the cloth hanging wetly against his trousers. She sobs a little, but the forces a laugh and leaves him.*

RUBY: Well! You'll think I'm a sook.

WILLIAM: You know what I think about you, Rube.

RUBY: Well you do it for us then. Try, even.

WILLIAM: Rube, all it'll depend on is them white fellers lettin' me have the chance. You don't worry about my bit, I cause there ain't nothin' I want so bad as to make us a good life family.

RUBY: You're a good man for wantin' it, Sweet William. No matter anythin' else comes.

WILLIAM: It'll be like I say, Rube. Just wait.

RUBY: I told you, fool man, we'll wait.

> *The door flies open and* PUMPKINHEAD *enters quickly, heading directly to unload coal from his shirt in front of the stove.*

Pumpkinhead!

PUMPKINHEAD: Arr, Mum. Gotcha some coal ... railway.

RUBY: [*with mixed feelings*] My good boy. Look at your bloody shirt.

WILLIAM: [*scoffing*] Railway!

> PUMPKINHEAD *gives him a filthy stare.* WILLIAM *weakens and shuts up.*

PUMPKINHEAD: [*playing the happy hunter*] Six lumps, Mum, keep you warm.

RUBY: Could I do without you? [*Giving him a quick hug, then complaining*] Oh you wicked boy, lookin' what you done to your clothes that I wash. Take 'em off, quick, and put your shorts on. Go get the bread ration.

> PUMPKINHEAD *grins and disappears to the bedroom.* RUBY *turns to* WILLIAM.

You shut up. I know ain't no railway coal left since years ago.

WILLIAM: [*a dig*] Thought stealin' was a sin.

RUBY: What stealin'? Hey? How's it you know, Sweet William, that maybe he ain't got a coal mine he's diggin' for himself? Clever boy like that …

WILLIAM: Wish he'd find a gold mine.

RUBY: Well, he might. But you leave him be, don't say nothin'll spoil what he thinks I think.

PUMPKINHEAD: [*entering in just a pair of shorts*] I'll run get the bread, Mum.

> *She smiles and nods. He goes out the door.* RUBY *goes off into the bedroom.*

SCENE FOUR

The garden of the MANAGER*'s nice white house on the mission. The door of the house has a few steps leading up to it. A large rubbish bin stands at the bottom of the steps, with a lid. Two men come out of the house. They are the* MANAGER *and the* INSPECTOR *of the mission, played by the same actors as the* PRIEST *and* SOLDIER *respectively. They pause in front of the house, chatting good-humouredly.*

INSPECTOR: Well, I must say Mrs Moreton really knows how to make scones.

MANAGER: She loved to hear you say so, Mr Gigg. Oh, yes, ha ha, she always says I married her for her scones.

> *They share a nice little laugh.*

INSPECTOR: Marvellous little housekeeper, always whenever I come to this mission, Mr Moreton, I'm always glad because I know your good wife will be here to set a civilised table, that, in your home, I'll find the sort of example that should be always shown to these poor devils that you're caring for, Yes indeed.

MANAGER: Thank you, Mr Gigg. I know I can speak for my good wife, too, that she'd appreciate your remark there.

INSPECTOR: Well, she's doing a fine job Now then, I suppose before it gets too late I'd better have a look about the place. Would you care to lead off?

MANAGER: Yes, well, we'll just poke about wherever the fancy takes us, eh? Make a few surprise raids? Ha ha!

INSPECTOR: Ha ha! Yes, catch 'em on the hop. Oh, ha ha!

They have fun considering their inspection. The CIVILIAN *stomps on. They pause, regarding him affably.*

MANAGER: Hello, sir.

CIVILIAN: You the trump around this rat's nest?

MANAGER: I beg your pardon?

CIVILIAN: Are you responsible, I mean, for keeping these black bastards on this reservation and away from decent people's property?

MANAGER: A mission, sir, not a reservation.

CIVILIAN: It's a rat's nest. Now, you listen to me, I'm only one of the people of this town who're sick and damn tired of your blacks and their thieving and damn vandalising and making a filthy nuisance of themselves around this town. And I'm here to see it stopped.

MANAGER: Well!

CIVILIAN: That's right! Damn right!

He stands there angrily. Pause.

MANAGER: Well, sir, Mr … ah … ?

CIVILIAN: Peterson.

MANAGER: Oh. How do you do?

They nod at each other. He indicates the INSPECTOR.

This is Mr Gigg.

The CIVILIAN *nods at the* INSPECTOR, *who nods.*

Mr Gigg is, ah, our Inspector, y'know, just about to have a look around the mission.

CIVILIAN: Yes? Well, then, I'd suggest he just has a look in their nests for half the private property in Cowra. Thieving, destroying, filthy nuisances I

MANAGER: [*tut-tutting*] Ho, now Mr Peterson! Really, it's plain you're rather upset, but do be a little more explicit.

CIVILIAN: Explicit?

INSPECTOR: Something to go on, you know.

CIVILIAN: Oh, something to go on, is it, you want? Well, then, a little while ago, you see, I went out into my own backyard—my own backyard—and just in time to catch the little animal at it again.

MANAGER: The little animal?

INSPECTOR: Doing what again?

CIVILIAN: At my coal box, pilfering it again, that's what the little animal was doing again. You know how many ton of coal he's got from my box this year?

MANAGER: Who?

CIVILIAN: The little black bastard who comes and takes it, of course! Aren't I telling you that?

MANAGER: Well! Mr Peterson, I—

CIVILIAN: Now, look! Let me say it another way. Look, your job is to run this ... this mission, right? Keep the black fellers two miles from the town, right? On this reservation, away from decent people and their property and their wives and their town, right?

MANAGER: Oh, well, in a way ... yes. But, you know, it's ...

CIVILIAN: Oh yes, I know! But do you know, do you know, that instead of doing your job sir, you're allowing them to run absolutely riot? Oh yes, staggering all over the town, around Cowra, drunk and filthy and an embarrassment to the whole community.

INSPECTOR: Drunk, you say?

CIVILIAN: Drunk. Filthy drunk. And it's getting so that decent women working in the shops simply dread to open their doors, for fear of the unpleasantness of having to refuse them credit, these drunken filthy blacks and their whining at the shop doors, stinking of metho, stinking of themselves, stinking the town out.

MANAGER: Well surely you exaggerate. I mean it's true we get complaints from time to time, but—

CIVILIAN: Hah! Time to time. It's all the time, blacks doing what they like all over Cowra. Not a day's work in the lot of 'em. What's the good of giving 'em welfare money, eh? What use, when all it does is load 'em with wine and metho and degrade a decent town?

MANAGER: That is not my responsibility, sir.

CIVILIAN: Oh, it isn't?

MANAGER: The Government pays out social service, Mr Peterson, not me. Nor would I, if you want to know, but in fact I've just got a job to do and I do it. I keep this mission clean.

CIVILIAN: Oh, you do?

MANAGER: Yes I do. The outside, at least.

CIVILIAN: Oh. Well, that's not good enough, not as from today. No, now look, I'm just a plain citizen and I want no part of running the affairs of men like yourself. No, that's right, but what I do want and what I am entitled to is your attention to your own job, you understand me?

What I mean is, I mean to say that all this that's been going on has to damn well stop and stop right now today.

INSPECTOR: [*making a note in his book*] Going on ...

MANAGER: Going on? What, uh, exactly ... ?

CIVILIAN: You know what I'm going to do? I'll tell you what I'm going to do. What I'm going to do, I'm going to hang a blasted rabbit trap where his black thieving hand comes through my gate to open it and steal my property. My coal! My wood! Anything that will burn, obviously, that his low-life parents send the little snake to thieve, obviously, in order to warm their blasted wigwams with my coal!

MANAGER: You've been missing some coal ...

CIVILIAN: Ah! I've been missing some coal! And what of the golf course, tell me that? What do you mean by their vandalism there? Tearing up the green ... And the gangs of 'en by the railway line, throwing rocks at decent people in their carriages. Not a fowl safe in its coop, not anywhere in the town or for twenty miles around! Our hens are stolen, our golf course destroyed, our fuel filched, our trees and gardens laid bare, sheep taken in broad daylight, goats, any damn thing dead or alive that they can eat, burn, or throw rocks at. Blasted lot of delinquent black baby bush rangers. Now what are you going to do?

MANAGER: The devil you say.

CIVILIAN: Yes exactly. The devil I say. Black bastards!

MANAGER: Well ...

INSPECTOR: Yes, well, we'll look into it.

CIVILIAN: Black bastards.

INSPECTOR: Oh quite. Quite, Mr Peterson.

CIVILIAN: I call a spade a spade.

INSPECTOR: Oh, ha ha ha ... that's very good.

MANAGER: Yes, Well I'll ...

CIVILIAN: Yes, well, I know you will ... what?

MANAGER: Well I'll investigate it. I'll ... enquire.

CIVILIAN: Oh you will?

MANAGER: Indeed I will.

CIVILIAN: Hmph. Yes, well, while you're doing that, I'll tell you what I'll be doing ... what every decent man in the town will be doing from now on.

MANAGER: Oh?

CIVILIAN: The next time I corner my particular piece of the Stone Age in my yard, well I'll be taking a gun and putting a bullet in his black arse. You hear?

Pause.

INSPECTOR: The next time you corner it—him?

MANAGER: You mean you already have ... caught him?

CIVILIAN: I had the little thief today, an hour ago. I told you that, he was there in my own yard.

MANAGER: Well, Mr Peterson, why on earth didn't you grab hold, take him in hand, and bring him to me?

CIVILIAN: [*pausing, horrified*] Take it in hand. D'you suggest that I'd actually touch one with my hands' Do you not know of their dirt, the lice of them? [*Scoffing*] I'd as soon dip me hands in the plague.

MANAGER: Yes, well ... well look. You say, sir, that you'd recognise your tormentor?

CIVILIAN: Would I!

INSPECTOR: Yes?

MANAGER: You would?

CIVILIAN: I would.

MANAGER: [*to the* INSPECTOR] He says he would.

INSPECTOR: Remarkable ... yes.

MANAGER: [*to the* CIVILIAN] Well perhaps you'd care then to accompany Mr Gigg and myself ... ?

CIVILIAN: Where to?

MANAGER: Mr Gigg is just about to inspect 'em.

CIVILIAN: What, all of 'em?

INSPECTOR: Oh no no no ... just here and there.

MANAGER: Never know, you might just see yours.

CIVILIAN: Right, well, I'll come then.

MANAGER: Good ... good ... well, let's away!

As they are about to leave, PUMPKINHEAD *arrives.*
Ah! It's Ruby's little fellow. What is it, then, my little man, your Mummy's bread, is it?
He takes the lid off the rubbish tin, gets out a loaf of bread and gives it to PUMPKINHEAD.
PUMPKINHEAD: Ta, boss.
He runs off with the bread. The CIVILIAN *does not recognise him.*
MANAGER: I dislike the way they all call me boss … [*Sighing*] Doesn't sound the best. Ah, well, Rome wasn't ruined in a day. Let's away then!
They walk off to inspect the mission. Faintly, off, we hear the kettle drum.

SCENE FIVE

RUBY'*s house.* WILLIAM *still hangs around in the room.* RUBY'*s at the stove. She puts down a pot, moving it from the heat to the side of the stove.*
RUBY: There, that's nice spinach.
She goes to set the table with spoon, syrup tin, and bowl of dripping for PUMPKINHEAD. *She returns to the pot, takes it from the stove and proceeds to the sink where she strains water from the spinach into a bowl. Then she puts the pot back on the side of the stove, leaving the bowl of spinach water on the side of the sink.*
There. Let that cool. Put some in the bottle for Bubby. Good for 'im.
WILLIAM: Oh Jesus. I got to do somethin', Rube.
He sits dejectedly on the upturned box.
RUBY: I hear Pumpkinhead.
She cocks her head, listening, and nods. PUMPKINHEAD *arrives back with the bread.*
PUMPKINHEAD: Y'are, Mum. Mr Moreton's around with that Mr Gigg, and there's a bad gubba with 'em.
WILLIAM: [*rising in some agitation and dismay*] Inspector?

PUMPKINHEAD: I got the bread and then sneaked back an' watched 'em. They comin' around the place, they are.

RUBY: Bad gubba? Who's a bad gubba?

PUMPKINHEAD: Ohhhh … I don' know 'im.

RUBY: How's he a bad gubba then?

PUMPKINHEAD: He's worse'n Mr Moreton. I know.

RUBY: They not comin' here, anyway. Now come on you sit down, boy, eat your good spinach up.

PUMPKINHEAD: [*pulling a face, but sitting at the table*] Ain' no good, spinach.

RUBY: Shut up. Eat.

She cuts some bread for him, spreads it with dripping and puts it by him. PUMPKINHEAD *starts to wolf the bread. She gets him a bowl of spinach. He pulls another face but eats it. She pours some spinach water into the syrup tin and takes it to him.*

Drink. All the goodness in it.

He sighs, nods and drinks some. There is a loud knock at the door. As RUBY *goes to answer, it is pushed open and the* MANAGER *and the* INSPECTOR *enter. The* CIVILIAN *pauses in the doorway.*

MANAGER: Well, Ruby. William. Here's Mr Gigg come along to see how we're going. Oh, come in, come in, Mr Peterson. [*Pulling him in*] Ruby, now this is Mr Peterson, from the town. He's paying us a visit. William, this is Mr Peterson.

WILLIAM: UM.

The CIVILIAN *gives a dirty nod. His eyes flick around the room. He sees the coal. The* INSPECTOR *snoops about slowly. He stands behind* PUMPKINHEAD *and pokes a couple of fingers in the boy's hair, prying and poking as* PUMPKINHEAD *squirms.*

INSPECTOR: [*satisfied*] Yesss … not too bad.

PUMPKINHEAD *scowls at the* INSPECTOR. *The* CIVILIAN *looks from the coal to the familiar scowl.*

CIVILIAN: Him. [*Pointing dramatically*] He's the one! [*Pointing to the coal*] And that's my coal. Right there.

He starts picking up his coal. PUMPKINHEAD *leaps up and fights him.*

PUMPKINHEAD: You leave that coal down.

He knocks the coal back on to the floor and kicking ferociously at the CIVILIAN *'S shins.*

That coal's my muvver's!

MANAGER: Hey hey hey! Enough of that!

He grabs PUMPKINHEAD *and shoves him away.*

RUBY: [*getting between the boy and men*] You leave that boy be!

INSPECTOR: Well!

CIVILIAN: My property. The coal is mine.

PUMPKINHEAD: Coal's not yours. Our coal!

CIVILIAN: Thief!

PUMPKINHEAD: [*scowling from behind* RUBY] Gubba! Git from our house!

MANAGER: Now, now, now! [*To* WILLIAM] William, it's quite obvious to me, and to Mr Gigg, that this coal belongs to Mr Peterson here. Plainly it was stolen, as Mr Peterson says, by this boy of yours. Now it must be returned at once.

I mean for a start … and then we'll have to see about this dreadful business of a boy from this mission stooping to theft.

He assumes a shocked air.

PUMPKINHEAD: [*to the* CIVILIAN] I send birriks on you now.

MANAGER: You be quiet, boy!

RUBY: Don' you tell my boy quiet! You callin' him thief then tellin' 'im be quiet soon's he don't like it! [*To the* CIVILIAN] You git! Git from my house! Sweet William, make 'im git!

They turn in a body to WILLIAM. WILLIAM *swallows nervously.*

WILLIAM: UM … well, you're doin' good, Rube

He nods his approval of her efforts. She is disappointed.

RUBY: You're sayin' it's your coal. How you knowin' it's your coal? You show me where it says on that coal it's your coal.

CIVILIAN: Ah! [*To the* MANAGER] It's my coal.

The INSPECTOR *'s roaming about. He opens cupboards and peers about here and there. The* MANAGER *hovers around after him. The* CIVILIAN *moves after them.*

Well, what are you going to do about it?

He sees past the INSPECTOR, *notes the empty cupboard. He frowns uncertainly, and begins to look around him, taking in the poverty of the place. His frown deepens.*

Good lord. What's all this?

The baby starts crying.

RUBY: Oh!

PUMPKINHEAD: Oreight, Mum.

PUMPKINHEAD gets the cloth. The visitors watch as he reaches into the cot with the cloth. The CIVILIAN *peers in.*

CIVILIAN: God!

PUMPKINHEAD: [*grimly*] No. It's Bubby.

The CIVILIAN's *eyes are widening. He turns to the* MANAGER, INSPECTOR *and* RUBY. *The crying stops.*

CIVILIAN: That's a baby …

He looks aghast at RUBY. *She nods silently.*

But, her eyes … What is it?

PUMPKINHEAD: Not her. Bubby's a him.

MANAGER: [*peering into the cot*] Ummm lot of that.

CIVILIAN: A lot? Where?

RUBY: [*gesturing to the mission outside*] Here.

The CIVILIAN *takes in the syrup tin and the remains of the spinach, bread and dripping. He looks more unhappy.*

CIVILIAN: God Almighty.

He moves a hand abruptly to his chest, as if a pain has struck him there. They all look at him and he looks at RUBY.

I've made a mistake. [*Shaking his head*] It's not my coal. Sorry. [*Nodding at the* MANAGER *and* INSPECTOR] It's not my coal.

He goes quickly to the door, turns to RUBY.

Sorry.

RUBY gives him a bemused nod.

PUMPKINHEAD: Told yuli.

CIVILIAN: Yes. I didn't see.

Abruptly he turns and is gone. Pause.

INSPECTOR: [*to the* MANAGER] Well!

MANAGER: I thought it was a heart attack.

They smile confusedly together.

RUBY: It was. That man just had little heart trouble.

PUMPKINHEAD: Pity it weren't big knock 'im sort.

MANAGER: Now, now! [*To the* INSPECTOR] Still ... most strange.

INSPECTOR: Um. Well there you are.

They shrug off the incident. Pause.

But, I'll still have to report this business, I'm afraid, soon as I get back to Sydney. [*Gesturing at the coal*] The point is, Ruby, William, it's my job to see things are in order here. This business of possible theft ...

MANAGER: [*nodding righteously*] I'll have to make a report myself.

They assure each other with righteous nodding.

It's a question of doing our jobs

INSPECTOR: Or of not doing our jobs.

MANAGER: That's what the whole point is.

INSPECTOR: Of course. The whole point.

They nod in unison at her.

RUBY: Oh.

INSPECTOR: But ...

[*Winking at* RUBY] Well, now, the other thing is this ... we have to consider

He pauses wisely. They wait on him.

I mean, now, I wouldn't want to be the sort of man who not willing to overlook one mistake. I mean every man, every boy, for that matter, as we all must agree, is entitle to a second chance. And, uh, the thing is, if I go back Sydney and report about a thief of a boy on this mission, well, the thing is that boy could easily end up being put in home for bad boys, you see, and we wouldn't want such thing to happen, would we? Over a boy's first mistake. So, ah ...

He pauses, regarding them.

RUBY: No. Man said the coal not his now.

PUMPKINHEAD: I never done it.

MANAGER: Well, I suppose not. Not the first time.

RUBY: Pumpkinhead won't do it no more. I promise.

INSPECTOR: No. Well ... [*warning*] but thieves are put in gaol, my boy, and other nasty places.

PUMPKINHEAD: Won't do it no more, Mr 'Spector.

INSPECTOR: [*looking satisfied*] Promise?

PUMPKINHEAD: My father's honour.

RUBY: He's promised.

MANAGER: Good boy.

INSPECTOR: [*pleased*] Ahhh ... father's honour! Ha ha, that's a new one. Very good too, yes.

> WILLIAM *looks pretty glum.*

What do you say, William? [*Joking*] When a boy swears on his father's honour, is that good enough for the world?

WILLIAM: Oh ...

> *He looks to* PUMPKINHEAD. PUMPKINHEAD'*s expression mocks him.*

RUBY: Good enough for me.

MANAGER: Good.

INSPECTOR: Yes, very good.

> *They make their fun, unaware of a conflict between* WILLIAM *and* PUMPKINHEAD.

Well, then, we'd best be getting along, Mr Moreton ...

> WILLIAM *has been trying to make up his mind on something. He does.*

WILLIAM: Mr Gigg, sir, 'fore you go ...

INSPECTOR: Yes ... ?

WILLIAM: [*hesitantly*] Mr Gigg ... don' wanna ask no favour to offend ...

INSPECTOR: Something I can do, William?

WILLIAM: Maybe, Mr Gigg. If— [*Suddenly firm*] Pumpkinhead, you run outside, play for little while while I talk somethin' with the grown-ups.

> *Pause.*

PUMPKINHEAD: Don't feel like playin'.

He turns his back on WILLIAM *and stands by* RUBY. WILLIAM *straightens his shoulders, moves quickly and plants the side of his boot against* PUMPKINHEAD'*s backside, knocking him to the floor.*

WILLIAM: [*firmly*] You play when I tell you.

PUMPKINHEAD *looks up, amazed and hurt. He feels his backside and appeals to* RUBY.

RUBY: You just heard your father, boy.

PUMPKINHEAD: [*scrambling up*] Ma!

WILLIAM: Out.

RUBY: Your father talkin' to you.

WILLIAM: [*waggling his boot suggestively*] Out.

RUBY: [*pushing him to the door*] G'wan, skit!

PUMPKINHEAD *goes out in miserable defeat.*

MANAGER: [*interested*] Well!

INSPECTOR: I hope this isn't a rude joke, William!

He cackles.

WILLIAM: No, sir, it's … Well, Mr Gigg, you said before you gonna go back down to Sydney soon—tomorrow?

INSPECTOR: Well yes, William.

WILLIAM: Me too?

INSPECTOR: You too?

WILLIAM: I got to go down to Sydney. [*Making it up*] Got a message, I did, Mr Gigg, my sister's awful sick and cryin' for me down there. Have to get down there soon's I ever can, 'fore she dies.

INSPECTOR: Oh?

He looks to RUBY. *She nods sadly.*

WILLIAM: I'm thinkin', Mr Gigg, won't mind if you say no, but I got to ask 'cause of m'sister …

INSPECTOR: You want a lift down, is that it?

WILLIAM: 'Zactly it.

INSPECTOR: Well of course. You know where you're going, I mean when you get there? Where is it?

WILLIAM: Town called Redfern, that's it. Suburb …

INSPECTOR: [*amused*] Ho, Redfern. Of course.

He exchanges a smile with the MANAGER.

WILLIAM: Well … got to get there.

INSPECTOR: All right. I'll take you there!

He nods and smiles in good humour.

WILLIAM: [*smiling*] You will? Tomorrow?

INSPECTOR: Leaving at noon.

WILLIAM: UM. Well, then what'll I do, Mr Gigg, I mean where will I come … to go?

MANAGER: Mr Gigg will be leaving from my house, William, you can find your way there all right.

INSPECTOR: Yes, that will do.

WILLIAM: [*nodding*] Twelve o'clock.

INSPECTOR: Have you in Sydney tomorrow evening. How will that do, not too late for you?

WILLIAM: Never too late, Mr Gigg.

He smiles at RUBY.

RUBY: [*nodding smugly*] Told you so.

INSPECTOR: And you'll be all right, Ruby, and the boy, while the man's away down there?

RUBY: Pumpkinhead'll mind us here.

MANAGER: I'll bet.

INSPECTOR: But who'll mind Pumpkinhead?

They take the excuse to end with a laugh. She goes to the door with them. They pause.

Twelve o'clock, William!

WILLIAM: I'll be there. Thanks.

INSPECTOR: Don't mention it. Bye, Ruby.

They go out together.

RUBY: [*softly*] Bye, 'Spector, Mr Moreton. [*Calling out the door*] Pumpkinhead? You come back now. [*Coming back to* WILLIAM] I'm gettin' your clothes pressed later, after Pumpkinhead's in bed and we talk.

WILLIAM: [*posing, the hunter about to go hunting*] Maybe I'll let 'im stay up.

RUBY: Oh. Well, if you say so, Sweet William.

She smiles. WILLIAM *smiles back at her.*

WILLIAM: Soon have you and him down after me, Rube, give you some surprise seein' what house you've got to live in. All the things we'll have then.

RUBY: You remember be careful, that's all, don't go forgettin' all what you said. Drinkin' ...

PUMPKINHEAD *enters. He prowls about, ignoring them.*

WILLIAM: [*loudly*] Well, no, course I won't, Rube! Soon as I get to Sydney ... [*eyeing* PUMPKINHEAD] tomorrow ... I'll be gettin' to see some brothers an' sisters, then sure I'll find out where's the work, and where's a red house with 'lectric light ... for us.

PUMPKINHEAD *turns, not believing his ears.*

RUBY: [*nodding to* PUMPKINHEAD] Your father's goin' to Sydney now, goin' down in the big car with Mr Gigg tomorrow.

Pause. PUMPKINHEAD *looks to* WILLIAM.

PUMPKINHEAD: Down there? [*Smiling*] Down Sydney?

WILLIAM: [*casually*] Arr, gettin' a good job, movin' you an' Mum an' Bubby down the city ... pretty soon.

PUMPKINHEAD: An' a red house ... you said.

WILLIAM: Um. New clothes an' things.

PUMPKINHEAD: Pretty soon?

WILLIAM: Um. Damn soon. You got to mind your mother for me an' Bubby ... an' hang on just a while.

PUMPKINHEAD *looks happily at* RUBY.

RUBY: I'll see where's some clothes, Sweet William, have to clean that suitcase in there.

She exits to the bedroom. WILLIAM *regards* PUMPKINHEAD.

WILLIAM: You'll do that ... be lookin' after things for me till I'm sendin' for you?

PUMPKINHEAD: Oh yeah.

He smiles at WILLIAM, *who smiles back and opens his arms.* PUMPKINHEAD *rushes to embrace him. Embarrassed,* WILLIAM *laughs and pushes the boy away lightly, then aims a playful jab at him.* PUMPKINHEAD *blocks it and throws a playful punch back. They box each other, laughing.*

WILLIAM: Jus' watch the ol' left, now.

He feints, and jabs a left, laughing. PUMPKINHEAD *boxes him back furiously* WILLIAM *suddenly surrenders, pretending to collapse from a blow. He lies, beaten.* PUMPKINHEAD *stands above him, fists in the air. They laugh.* WILLIAM *reaches up and pulls* PUMPKINHEAD *down. They sit pushing each other happily.* RUBY *enters, sees them and smiles.*

RUBY: Well!

She grins and leaves again. Pause.

WILLIAM: Now you don' get in no trouble, not now.

PUMPKINHEAD: No.

WILLIAM: Anythin' you've stole, you put it back … you do that? [*Nodding*] An' let me get us things.

PUMPKINHEAD: [*reluctant, then nodding*] Yeah.

WILLIAM: Like that coal. You put it back.

PUMPKINHEAD: UM. [*Sighing*] You say so, Dad.

WILLIAM *nods that he does say so.*

ACT THREE

SCENE ONE

Next afternoon. The CIVILIAN'*s backyard. The scene is as before, except that on the coal bin sits a large deep box filled with goodies: groceries packed high; all sorts of packets and bottles, etcetera. The small black hand comes through the gate and slips the bolt.* PUMPKINHEAD *pushes the gate open, pokes his head in and enters the yard. He carried the coal in a small hessian bag. He proceeds quietly towards the coal bin, then pulls up, staring in astonishment at the box of groceries. He is confused because the box is on the coal bin, preventing him from lifting the lid; then he is tempted. He hesitates, then shakes his head at himself. He takes the pieces of coal from his bag one at a time laying them in front of the bin. Holding the empty bag, he picks out a few articles from the box. He fights off the devil reluctantly, trudges slowly to the gate and, after a lingering look at the groceries, leaves. Pause. The* CIVILIAN *appears quietly from the house. He looks with surprise at the groceries and at the returned coal. He runs after* PUMPKINHEAD, *and stands in the gate calling after him.*

CIVILIAN: Hey, wait a minute! Come back. Boy! Come on. I won't hurt you. Come on, here. [*Coaxing*] Want to show you …

> *He nods and steps back to allow the returning* PUMPKINHEAD *into the yard.* PUMPKINHEAD *pauses inside the gate, pointing.*

PUMPKINHEAD: Din' take nothin'. See? Put it back …
CIVILIAN: No, come on, that's for you. Take it now.

> *He points to the goodies.* PUMPKINHEAD *looks astonished and confused.*

Take it to y.our mother. Go on.

> *Lifting the box, offering it to* PUMPKINHEAD.

I mean it, go on, take it.

PUMPKINHEAD *nods. He smiles a little. He tries to pick up the box. It is much too big and heavy.*

Oh. [*Gesturing*] Go on, get that end … out the gate now … I'll show you, just out here … we'll get it in the car … lift it up now …

PUMPKINHEAD *grins in astonishment, but he lifts.*

Right. Now you walk backwards.

They tote the box between them out the gate. The yard stands empty again. A car door slams, off. A motor starts up.

SCENE TWO

RUBY *'s house. The table is bare.* RUBY *Sits in her chair reading, of course, her Bible. The door is knocked open and* PUMPKINHEAD *comes in backwards with one end of the box, the* CIVILIAN *following on the other end.*

PUMPKINHEAD: Mum! Look, Mum!

Poor RUBY, *she stands and drops the Good Book.* PUMPKINHEAD *and the* CIVILIAN *stand smiling with the box.*

CIVILIAN: Where do you want it? It's for you.

RUBY, *speechless, indicates the table.*

Right. Lift it, boy.

They heave the box on to the table. RUBY *and the* CIVILIAN *stand there looking at each other. He shrugs, indicating the box. His tone asks acceptance.*

It's just some things …

RUBY: [*solemnly*] That's … you're kind.

Pause.

CIVILIAN: Well, you see … I didn't know.

RUBY *nods, and she smiles a little smile.*

PUMPKINHEAD: [*dying to get at the box*] We gonna see?

He looks from RUBY *to the box.*

CIVILIAN: Why, sure we're gonna see! [*Ruffling the boy's head, and pointing at the box*] Come on, let's get it out of there.

He begins to pull everything from the box. He gives each item to PUMPKINHEAD, *who grins wider and wider, accepting each item, grinning at* RUBY, *piling things on the table. The scene is a very excited and happy one.* RUBY, *hesitating, picks up a big tin of milk, looks at it, smiles, looks at the cot, smiles. The box is emptied, apparently, and the* CIVILIAN *lifts it off the table, puts it on floor reaches in.*

And last, but not least ...

He pulls out a cardboard box.

PUMPKINHEAD: [*eagerly*] What's it?

CIVILIAN: [*winking*] Ah, ha!

He opens it and lifts out a great big cake, which he puts on the table. PUMPKINHEAD*'s eyes open wide. He stares open mouthed at the* CIVILIAN, *at the cake, at* RUBY, *and points suddenly in recognition.*

PUMPKINHEAD: [*awed*] Awwww! You d'Cake Man!

The CIVILIAN *smiles. He looks to* RUBY *in puzzlement.* RUBY *smiles at him and nods to* PUMPKINHEAD.

Cake Man!

He rushes at the CIVILIAN, *embracing him excitedly. The* CIVILIAN *hugs him back, pleased and affectionate.*

Got to tell Collie! [*Dancing happily*] Got to tell Noelie! Tell 'em all!

He runs out the door. His voice can be heard screeching, off.

Hey, Collie, the Cake Man! Found the Cake Man! Noelie! Cake Man! Robbie! Come on, come an'see what's in here. The Cake Man!

The CIVILIAN, *looks puzzled, smiling, at* RUBY. *She shrugs. They both look to the door, and kids come streaming in the door one after another as* PUMPKINHEAD *shows them the cake, the big, beautiful cake, and the 'Cake Man', who has trouble embracing all those kids as they run to him.* RUBY *gives him a knife. He gives cake to all the children.*

SCENE THREE

This scene could be a brief film sequence. Evening. A street in Redfern, outside a pub. We hear traffic, a juke box from the pub, voices and laughter and all the pub noises. SWEET WILLIAM *walks along quietly and stands outside the pub door. He has a battered suitcase in his hand. He pauses, looking in. Out the door staggers a drunk. He is an Aborigine. A few others like him are pushed out the door. The* PUBLICAN *appears behind them in the doorway.*

PUBLICAN: Now g'wan get on your way! Back when you're sober.

> *They mutter and mumble and call abuse. They bump into* SWEET WILLIAM *and crowd about him.*

Go on, piss off. [*Warning*] The police were rung for five minutes ago. Better get.

> *They give him some more abuse, and linger. We hear the roar of a police van pulling up. The* PUBLICAN *nods. The Kuris look on in alarm. Two* POLICEMEN *run on with batons.*

POLICEMAN: This the trouble, Mr Pott?

> *The* PUBLICAN *nods. He turns and goes inside his pub. The* POLICEMEN *proceed to arrest the lot. They run them off to the van, and at last the pair rush back at* SWEET WILLIAM.

Right you, get your arse in that wagon.

WILLIAM: Who, me? Oh, no boss, I'm down from the bush.

POLICEMAN: Don't you bloody well answer me back!

> *They grab* WILLIAM. *They give him the bum's rush offstage. We hear the wagon door being slammed and locked. Doors slam. The motor starts, roars and fades. The* PUBLICAN *appears in door. He smiles, satisfied after the wagon. Music: 'There's a Happy Land Somewhere'.*

EPILOGUE

SWEET WILLIAM *enters, in different clothes, and speaks DIRECTLY to the audience.*

WILLIAM: NO? Ah, well it don't matter. Please don't give it another thought. Forget all that shit they say about giving me back my culture. That's shit. It isn't what I'm really after, not really. What I want, what I'm here for … it's something else again, if I could get it across what I mean …

Pause. He sits down.

Look, I'll tell you something. No laughing, you're not allowed to laugh but you got to try and listen and not call me a liar or laugh. I'm no liar … ask Ruby, ask my missus, she'll tell you that's one thing about me, that I ain't a liar … one thing I'm not.

Pause.

You ever heard of eurie-woman? You say it like that, eurie-woman. No? Never heard of one 'a them? Well, listen, then. I'll tell you what's a eurie-woman, and what it is I want here.

I was working at Killara Station … after I had me feed, I went an' laid down on me bed an' started readin' this gubba book I had … [*wide-eyed*] … an' all of a sudden I heerd this emu drummin' somewhere close, I got up and wen' outside an' stocked up the fire, and all the time this emu was still drummin'. I's trying to hear 'zactly where it was so I could find that nest … then the drummin' started closer to the tent. I was sort of curious, like, y'know?

Pause.

I thought I won't have no trouble finddin' that nest vin the mourning … but this time it was right behind the tent.

Pauses dramatically.

Sooooo … while I was turnin' round I got the biggest fright of me whole fuckin' life! I weren't no emu it was a woman. And she had hair that was shinin' black, an' it hung down over her backside. She was the prettiest woman I ever saw … yeah … she was a eurie-woman … I fair bolted out of there! You'da thought I had wings, the way I flew out a there … [*shaking his head slowly*] didn' do no good, must have run easy a mile … but just as I ducked through the fence wires, there she was again, right in front of a man … between me an' the road … an' it was summer, hot as fuckin' hell but I had the freezin' cold sweat all over me … an' then I took off again, runnin' for my life, scairter than ever I was before … runnin' fast … but didn't matter hoe or where, she was always there in front of me, and at the same distance away from me her hair shinin' and swirling like it was made out of water, an' her skin like black lightin' if you can imagine that … so beautiful she couln' even be bad … but she was scary anyway, an' always there in front of me … but somewhere else.

He pauses in reverie.

Well, all I remember then is a gubba I was workin' for, was sayin' to me what was wrong what happened … an' just the way he looked at me I knew he never had, that he never would or never could see that eurie-woman… a gubba. Ain't no eurie-woman for Gubbas, she came to tell me so I'd know.

Pause.

[*Smiling*] Y'know what? He said: 'Come on, William, ain't no eurie-woman … come back to reality.'

Pause.

[*Smiling sadly*] Exac'ly what that eurie-woman was sayin' to me …

Pause.

Two realities.

Pause.

An' I've lost one.

Pause.

Bit I want it back … I need it back.

Pause.

Not yours … mine.

THE END

www.ingramcontent.com/pod-product-compliance
Lightning Source LLC
Chambersburg PA
CBHW050019090426
42734CB00021B/3334